I0052029

PRAISE FOR REIMAGINING HEALTHCARE

"Douglas has amazing insights into the challenges facing the healthcare system today, not just from the perspectives of an expert clinician, but that of a patient, a consumer and someone with business and organisational acumen."

—Ms Rosina Hislop, Board Director
& Governance Consultant

"Having managed healthcare in both private and public sectors for the last 20 years, I echo the observations and analyses put forward by Dr Fahlbusch and I look forward to the results when his proposed solutions and interventions are implemented."

—Professor Steevie Chan, The
University of Notre Dame, Australia

"Having worked as a supply chain and procurement specialist for the past 30 years, I have experienced firsthand the difficulties faced in private hospitals in Australia. This book is a must-read for decision-makers in healthcare."

—Mr Len Kennedy, Len Kennedy
Healthcare Solutions

"Imagine... healthcare where patients, clinicians and administrators collaborate with the one goal 'to improve the healthcare system'. What if we also included technology to achieve these objectives? Impossible? No. It is entirely possible. Douglas Fahlbusch's book *Reimagining Healthcare* shows not just how this is possible, but more importantly *why*. If you wish to improve the outcomes for your patients, this book is a must read."

—Ms Julie Misson, author of *Make It Appen*: *Planning and designing an app to enhance patient care*

"This book will challenge your thinking about the type of behaviours and traits we need to meet the demands facing healthcare. Although we have elements of collaboration, healthcare is still in silos. Now we have the opportunity to create an engaging model of care that can inspire and drive change with true patient centricity, improved patient outcomes, and a healthcare model that is sustainable."

—Mr Arthur Mitsioulis, Managing Director, OPIS HEALTHCARE

REIMAGINING HEALTHCARE

**How clinicians and non-clinicians
reduce risk, waste and disjointed services**

DR DOUGLAS FAHLBUSCH

DoctorZed
Publishing
www.doctorzed.com

Copyright © by Douglas Fahlbusch 2019

Creative commons license. Reimagining Healthcare by Douglas Fahlbusch is licensed under a Creative Commons Attibution Non-commercial Share-Alike 4.0 International License and is based on work at www.douglasfahlbusch.com. Permissions beyond the scope of this license are available at www.douglasfahlbusch.com.

Copies of this book can be ordered via the author's website at www.douglasfahlbusch.com, booksellers or by contacting:

DoctorZed Publishing
10 Vista Ave, Skye,
South Australia 5072
www.doctorzed.com

ISBN: 978-0-6482118-0-8 (hc)
ISBN: 978-0-6485361-9-2 (sc)
ISBN: 978-0-6485361-8-5 (e)

A CiP number is available at the National Library of Australia.

Because of the dynamic nature of the Internet, any web addresses or links contained in this book may have changed since publication and may no longer be valid. The views expressed in this work are solely those of the author and do not necessarily reflect the views of the publisher, and the publisher hereby disclaims any responsibility for them.

The author of this book does not dispense medical advice or prescribe the use of any technique as a form of treatment for physical, emotional, or medical problems without the advice of a physician, either directly or indirectly. The intent of the author is only to offer information of a general nature. In the event you use any of the information in this book for yourself, which is your constitutional right, the author and the publisher assume no responsibility for your actions.

Printed in Australia, UK and USA

DoctorZed Publishing rev. date: 31/10/2019

CONTENTS

With heartfelt thanks to my wife Liz, my children Hugo and Sarah, and my clinical and non-clinical colleagues, without whom this would not have been possible.

PREFACE

"Never doubt that a small group of thoughtful committed citizens can change the world. Indeed, it is the only thing that ever has."
– Margaret Mead

Collaboration trumps genius. The remixing of ideas creates insights. Collaboration and insights unlock innovation. Cognitive diversity is key to more expansive remixing of ideas, broader collaborative efforts, and greater insights. Cognitive diversity arises from systemic and individual factors, such as different training systems, cultures, gender and personal preferences.

Innovation thus comes from standing on the shoulders of others, allowing us to reach ever higher. This is how change occurs and accelerates, and is why and how we will be able to reimagine and reinvent healthcare.

"If each part of a system, considered separately, is made to operate as efficiently as possible, the system as a whole will not operate as effectively as possible."
– Russell Ackoff

ACKNOWLEDGEMENTS

I would like to acknowledge contributions from many interviews with clinical and non-clinical people, my publisher and colleague Dr Scott Zarcinas, reviewers Mr Len Kennedy (www.lenkennedyhealthcaresolutions.com), Ms Julie Misson (www.makeitappen.com.au) and Mr Arthur Mitsioulis (www.opishealthcare.com.au), Industry Leaders Fund (industryleaders.com.au), Dent Global (www.dent.global), Entrepreneurs Organisation (www.eonetwork.org), Growth Institute (www.growthinstitute.com), Mr Dave Chase (www.healthrosetta.org), the Grattan Institute (www.grattan.edu.au), The King's Fund (www.kingsfund.org.uk), Mr Graham Andrewartha (www.mcpheeandrewartha.com.au), my editor Ms Hari Teah, and a healthcare system that saved me from the death that would have been certain only a few short generations ago.

FOREWORD

In this book, *Reimagining Healthcare: How clinicians and non-clinicians reduce risk, waste and disjointed services*, Dr Douglas Fahlbusch highlights many of the contentious issues that face physicians, hospital administrators, health fund providers, and governments with the difficult, multifaceted problem of delivering cost-effective healthcare. As a result, the patient, who ought to be the beneficiary of all efforts, is left stranded, helpless and cheated.

But it doesn't have to remain that way. Dr Fahlbusch shows patients, carers, healthcare providers, funders, and regulatory bodies how to collaborate by using his six-step process. By taking these steps, all stakeholders in healthcare can provide treatment that is efficient, systematic and adaptable to accommodate not only the current needs, but the new wants and needs for all involved.

Len Kennedy, Len Kennedy
Healthcare Solutions

INTRODUCTION

'I have enjoyed great satisfaction from my climb of Everest and my trips to the poles. But there's no doubt that my most worthwhile things have been the building of schools and medical clinics.'

Sir Edmund Hillary

Healthcare is dying. The lifeblood of healthcare, to help and heal people, has been trickling away for a long time. Healthcare is the only industry that involves everyone at one time or another. However, meaningful, values-based healthcare is dying a slow, painful death, and we need to help it regain a strong heart.

For many countries, healthcare is the largest government expenditure. Increasingly, healthcare is designed around its providers rather than its patients or its purpose. Supply and demand often change according to availability, rather than medical need. Poor morale, burnout and depression are reaching record levels. The healthcare system is more often isolating, rather than collaborative. I believe that to jump-start healthcare's heart, we need clinicians and administrators to help each other remember the 'why' of healthcare. By using the non-clinical aspects of healthcare delivery, the 'business', as a clinical tool we can restore the primary purpose of healthcare, to ensure the exchange of value is between patient and provider[1].

SOME BACKGROUND

I have a great life as a medical specialist. 'So' I hear you say, 'Why don't you just stay comfortable being an anaesthetist?' It's because I see first-hand the effects of the increasingly complex healthcare system on both patients and staff. As well as being a medical professional, I'm also a patient, so I've experienced the gaps in healthcare, the frustrations of receiving limited information and options, and the effects of this on family and friends. I am an insider, and can only imagine how bewildering the healthcare system is to most patients.

Through my work I optimise patients before operations, look after them while they are asleep, and optimise their recovery. This means that I interact with staff, patients and healthcare facilities at many points in a patient's care journey. I constantly see pockets of excellence, separated by paper walls that block the flow of care, impair the patient and healthcare staff experience, and perpetuate increased risk and cost in the delivery of healthcare - blocks that shouldn't be there.

THE HEALTHCARE BRAIN

I've always been interested in thinking about systems and solving complex problems, particularly where there are competing requirements. This describes healthcare – it's like a brain with a clinical side, and a business administration side. However, these two sides don't communicate efficiently. This leads to intense bursts of activity that are poorly coordinated to the circumstances or intended outcomes, much as it does in a human with this condition. In a human it is termed corpus callosum deficiency, and leads to attention deficit behaviour and hyperactivity.

My role in anaesthesia, to reconcile the competing requirements of a patient, their diseases and the operation that they are about to undergo, has ignited a desire to reconcile the business requirements for healthcare delivery with the clinical needs. I have a background in dealing with large and inflexible bureaucracies, most notably the military. I have become disconcerted to see that the healthcare bureaucracy has some similarities in terms of how dehumanising it can be. This is deliberate when preparing people for the rigours of warfare. However, it is unintended in healthcare and creates unwanted adverse outcomes.

BUSINESS AS A CLINICAL TOOL

An early insight on how to solve the complex problems of healthcare came ten years ago, when I was volunteering on state and national committees for the Australian Medical Association and the Australian Society of Anaesthetists. I realised that as a doctor I did not speak the language of business, and that business people don't speak the language of healthcare. This means that a lot of value is being lost in translation, to the detriment of both health outcomes and business outcomes. In order to bridge this gap, I went on to study a Graduate Diploma in Management so that I would be conversant in both 'languages'. The insights I gained were terrific for improving my anaesthesia practice, and of great benefit to the patients and nurses that I interact with as well. Putting people first and processes second resulted in better outcomes.

Already pleased with the results of this newfound knowledge, the real turning point came seven years ago when I became a patient. I thought I had a common and minor complaint, which was possibly being over-investigated. It turned out to be something more sinister than I had expected, and I was diagnosed with cancer. Lying alone in corridors with only a thin sheet for protection, I had plenty of time to think. Wouldn't it be great if the system worked in such a way that it helped to improve healthcare, instead of relying on patients, doctors and staff to constantly make up for the system's short-comings?

BARRIERS

Why is reducing the risks and costs in healthcare, and improving the experience of it, such a struggle? My view is that it's because healthcare has become highly complex, but the model for delivering healthcare hasn't changed. Healthcare has grown exponentially since its provider-centric beginnings. In other complex industries, it is no longer an individual in charge, whether building a skyscraper, running an airport, or controlling an oil and gas installation. In past generations, one person could oversee these operations. However, they were much smaller than the operations of today without the myriad systems required - electrical, electronic, hydraulic, engineering and so on. This complexity requires collaborative teams for effective delivery.

Healthcare is no different. However, we persist with a system that has administrators and care-providers working and optimising their systems independently of one another, like a disconnected brain. We need a system that supports collaboration, so that the outcome is a coordinated and efficient healthcare system that benefits patients – rather than itself, or worse just individual parts of itself.

Because solving the risk, cost and availability problems of healthcare appears too hard, we focus on piecemeal projects. These projects have the desired effect of reducing visible problems, such as infection or leg clots. However, they unintentionally increase the complexity of delivering healthcare. They bring new problems, such as decreased efficiency due to duplication of effort, wasted time and materials, and stress on staff. We wonder why the improved parts don't lead to an improved whole. The clinical side of healthcare delivery tends to blame the business side, and the business side tends to blame the clinical. How do we reconcile these seemingly conflicting demands?

WHAT DOESN'T WORK

When I completed the graduate diploma of management, I saw that successful businesses ensure an exchange of value by putting the customer first. Businesses that falter put other objectives first, most commonly money. A good example is Apple – when it started it was about designing products for people. In the 90's, Apple management lost that DNA and the company nearly failed. When its founder, Steve Jobs, was brought back in the 2000's the focus turned once again to designing products for people - and success returned. When Microsoft changed its culture from combative to collaborative in 2010, its commercial success increased considerably. These companies are now the most valuable companies in the US, if not the world[2].

For a healthcare example in Australia, private hospital systems in the 1980's became profit-focused, instead of purpose-focused. A number of hospitals failed. As well as demonstrating the importance of an enterprise's purpose, this example also helps explain the antipathy between the clinical and business sides of healthcare delivery[3].

A WAY FORWARD

So how do we apply these lessons to fixing healthcare? We know that we need the expertise of clinical care providers, and that the complexity of healthcare means that we also need business expertise. What is lacking is collaboration between the two; what is needed is a system that builds the trust and teamwork to make it happen. This is where I have focused my efforts. This book summarises methods that optimise the patient care journey, reduce waste of labour and materials, and improve the experience of healthcare for patients, staff and doctors. This helps to ensure benefit for all involved.

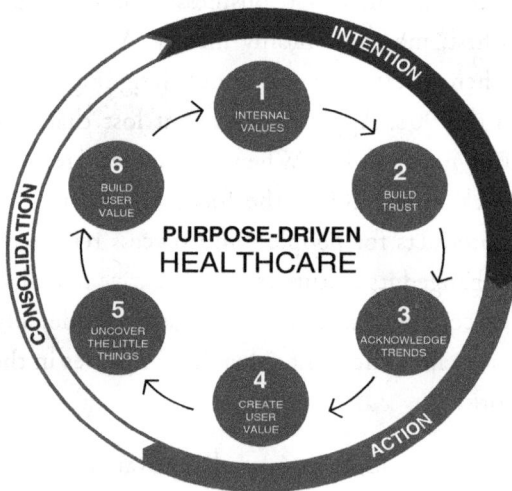

FIGURE 1   Six-Step Method

Figure 1 illustrates how using clinical and business experience helps healthcare staff to identify improvement projects that make their lives easier, and patients' experiences better. These purposeful projects reduce clinical risk and improve clinical outcomes. In doing so, staff engagement and efficiency increase, and the projects satisfy business improvement requirements such as reducing cost and meeting compliance mandates. Healthcare facilities become preferred providers and employers, with enviable reputations, referrals and revenues.

Healthcare's current delivery models are unsustainable, and are a knife in the heart of healthcare. Combining excellent healthcare delivery with robust business processes reverses this trend and ensures that healthcare remains accessible to all. The collaboration models that this requires promote engagement and efficiency, and systematise adaptability to accommodate new wants and needs for all involved: patients, carers, healthcare providers, funders and regulatory bodies.

Thank you for reading this book. I want you to be part of 'healing healthcare', and of restoring its healthy heartbeat, so that everyone can have access to care wherever and whenever they need.

Main Points:

1. Healthcare delivery and budgets are in trouble
2. Healthcare relies on clinical delivery and business capability – however these domains of expertise rarely collaborate
3. Lack of collaboration results in mismatch between effort and outcome
4. Collaboration reduces cost and risk, and increases quality
5. Improvement needs to come from within

WHY

1 WHERE IS HEALTHCARE GOING?

'If you have to go to the hospital, we have failed you'
Aetna CEO Mark Bertolini

We are all aware of the funding pressures facing healthcare. There are also social demands for more information, more inclusion, more caring. And there are massive technological changes affecting the nature of communities, work and play. I believe these pressures will result in a transition from healthcare's current model of reacting to disease ('disease-care'), to a new model of the proactive optimisation of health ('health-care'), that reduces the burden of disease and optimises individuals' quality of life and productivity.

The wide reach and low cost of service delivery via technology makes this change possible. Social demands make it almost inevitable. It means designing healthcare delivery around the patient and their data, and making it easy, cheap and safe for patients and healthcare staff to access healthcare information and services on demand, where and when required.

THE CASE FOR CHANGE

We accept that healthcare is too important to ignore. It is a fundamental need, like food and shelter. However, it is the least well-designed, least well-organised sector of our economy, and the last to benefit from the information age. Global spending on healthcare is US$8.1 trillion (A$11.1 trillion) with 5-10%

growth per annum. Despite being described as the greatest current threat to the US economy, it is 'too important to change' and continues without reaching its full potential. Many improvement programmes have foundered on the rocks of good intentions. This includes technology – multiple failures suggest that 'healthcare is where technology startups go to die'[1-3].

Improvements in service which are now standard in the financial sector include anywhere/anytime access to one's personal information. However, in healthcare there are three components; clinical, which is optimising the medical knowledge and processes; administrative, which is optimising the infrastructure and non-medical processes; and their interaction – 'the system'. The first two spend little time planning or practicing the system together in the interests of the patient. This narrow, siloed focus means it's no surprise that healthcare isn't optimised systemically and falls over on efficiency and outcome measures.

Healthcare is Australia's single biggest pressure on government budgets. Australian hospitals provided 10.6 million admissions, and 33.4 million non-admitted services in 2016. Healthcare is also Australia's biggest industry, at A$150 billion or 12.7% of GDP, with over 1.5 million persons employed in healthcare and social assistance. In addition to the size of the sector, there are multiple interdependent participants in healthcare delivery. Healthcare has customers (patients), employees, independent players (healthcare providers), suppliers of equipment, pharmaceuticals and consumables, infrastructure (e.g. hospitals), and funders (government and private insurers) [4-6].

To add to the complexity, external pressures include aging

populations, increasing complexity of disease and treatments, obesity, technology, and consumer demands. 14.4% of the Australian population is over 65, compared with 25.2% Japan, 21.1% Germany, 14.1% USA, 10% Singapore and 9.7% China. Australia's elderly population is expected to double in one generation[7].

WHAT ARE THE TRENDS?

Consequently, the trend for healthcare availability, accessibility and affordability is downward. In contrast, electronic interconnectedness means that availability, accessibility and affordability for most other things in our lives are increasing. Whether it be lifestyle, wellness, education, or media, 'there is an app for that'. Patients compare the ease and simplicity of interacting with the financial sector, which is available online to them 24/7, with the confusion, duplication and paper-driven nature of the healthcare sector. Healthcare is generally only available when visiting a healthcare professional, and even then availability, accessibility and affordability are often incomplete.

ARE WE HAPPY?

At the same time, deteriorating work and life satisfaction in industrialised nations is leading to greater understanding that humans are not simple transactional beings. We are human beings, not human 'doings'. That is to say, humans desire to be a part of a greater purpose, beyond the day-to-day mechanics of existence. This is important both emotionally and economically, as it leads to out-performance through a 'whole being greater than the sum of its parts' effect. Healthcare, however, is rooted in a transactional model that prevents out-performance, or the possibility of reducing cost of care while increasing quality of care. Staff appear to be hanging on in quiet desperation in order to meet documentation and compliance requirements, while continuing to help patients[8, 9].

Part of the transactional model involves siloed service-delivery. That is, healthcare is provider-centric, whether a hospital, clinic or a clinician. In healthcare, information is maintained in silos based around hospitals, clinics and clinicians, and consumers have difficulty informing the conversation. This results in unhappy patients, resigned to poor service because 'that's the way healthcare is'. Staff become hardened to the patient experience, creating a production line rather than a personalised experience[10-12].

When healthcare talks about being patient-centred, it is designed and operated in a siloed healthcare provider/organisation-centred way. Other industries have abandoned silo thinking in favour of systems thinking, with innovative teams rather than individual experts solving customers' problems. Compare accessing healthcare with transport (airlines, Uber), online shopping (Amazon, Ebay), knowledge (Google, Wikipedia, media), accommodation (Airbnb) and the financial sector (online banking and investing). These present their experiences in a user focussed way.

WHO REALLY PAYS?

While Australian expenditure on healthcare as a proportion of GDP is comparable to most westernised nations, the fastest growing expense in the household budget is healthcare. This is due to the patient contribution, or 'out-of-pocket' expense that occurs when healthcare is accessed. A double whammy of rebates to patients from health funds and Medicare increasing below inflation, combined with fees for services and products increasing at or above inflation means that health payers cover less and less of the cost of healthcare every year. These expenses are both clinical (e.g. medications, equipment, healthcare worker fees) and non-clinical (e.g. transport, time off work to access services, duplication of effort and so on). This impacts on education, quality of food and accommodation, and retirement savings at the household level[13].

Health is the biggest pressure on government budgets overall

Change in Australian governments' expenditure 2003-2014
$ bn relative to CPI

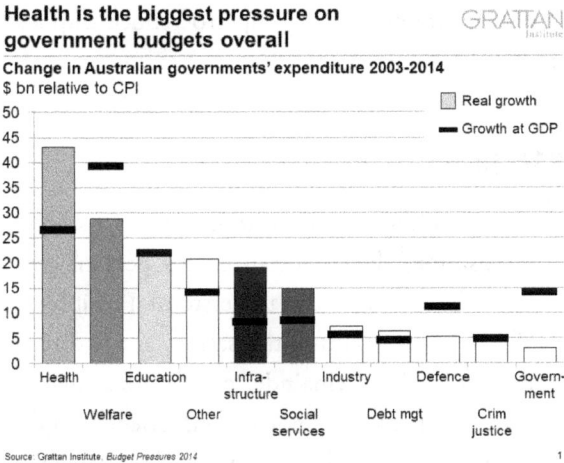

Source: Grattan Institute, Budget Pressures 2014

FIGURE 2   Healthcare Cost Pressures

As shown by Figure 2 above, the biggest funding pressure on government is healthcare. Until recently, cost control has centred around restricting access to products and services to encourage 'needs-based' healthcare rather than 'wants-based'.

Unfortunately, this often affects those most in need, and those least able to access healthcare via their own means. With deterioration in health comes an increase in need for services – and a decrease in the ability to be self-sufficient. Chronic disease is a large area of cost; for example, kidney failure, heart failure and diabetes[14].

Encouragingly, the conversation at a national level has turned to a more strategic approach, centred around delivering healthcare to the population in a more coordinated way. Rather than perpetuating today's splintered approach to segments such as acute and aged care, community and hospital care, medical and allied healthcare and so on, coordinated care looks for commonalities among these groups to reduce duplication of effort and healthcare errors[15].

WHERE TO, THEN?

As part of healthcare's transition from disease-care to health-optimisation, the importance of a person's context to their disease is becoming better understood. Possibly only 20% to 30% of a person's health-optimisation comes directly from modern healthcare. The remainder comes from environmental factors such as personal motivation, friends and family, socio-economic status and geographical location (Figure 3). Social, psychological, and biological information imports have been made possible with sensors and information networks that didn't exist as little as five years ago. Technology now allows us to analyse and take advantage of these new sources of information, provide information and guidance to healthcare workers and users remotely, and to encourage active participation of patients in their treatment through feedback.

The future health ecosystem will focus on
the true drivers of outcomes

FIGURE 3   Social Determinants of Health

Processing of this additional information is ideally performed by technology. Similarly, performance of repetitive low value tasks is ideally suited to technology. Augmented reality and artificial intelligence provide tools today that were theoretical a few short years ago. Technology allows us to off-load cognitive demand that threatens to overwhelm humans on the one hand, while expanding the reach of care-providers across time and geography on the other. Care-givers and patients can focus on the interactions to which we are best adapted – human-to-human, as distinct from human-to-paper or human-to-computer[16, 17].

Augmented reality and artificial intelligence help to address three macroeconomic changes highlighted above: 1) aging of the population (workforce and patients); 2) deskilling outside of metropolitan centres as populations migrate to cities; and 3) more sophisticated machines in rural and remote locations alongside growing healthcare system complexity. Connecting people and data provides the tools to help address social demands for more collaboration and self-determination in care. Healthcare is moving away from hospitals ('disease-care') into the community, and increasingly occurring outside the regulated healthcare delivery model[18, 19].

WHAT ABOUT THE HUMANS?

Rather than depersonalising care, high-tech healthcare frees people up to strengthen the uniquely human aspects of their interactions. How do we use this to make healthcare safer, cheaper and a better experience for everyone involved? By picking discrete, measurable projects where we can understand all of the associated costs and benefits, we can improve healthcare delivery. Smoothing the patient journey through the healthcare system is one such method. It is a complete system of need, intervention, outcome and feedback. For the patient journey, or 'Patient Flow', to avoid the eddies and turbulence that we see today, users of the healthcare system - patients and care-givers - need to be at its centre. Work flows and work processes need to connect and support people, with technology playing a big part in promoting collaboration and the de-siloing of people and processes. The Virginia Mason Medical Centre in Seattle is one such site – error rates have fallen as efficiency has increased, and the patient experience ratings have improved markedly[20].

I believe that both healthcare providers of treatment and managers of infrastructure need to think in a similar fashion about healthcare as a system. A powerful common outcome goal is to improve the patient experience, as the patient is the one factor present throughout a treatment programme. This approach is used successfully by the International Consortium for Health Outcomes Measurement (http://www.ichom. org/). However, I would go a step further, and say that we should improve both the patient's *and* the healthcare worker's experience. Collaboration paves the way for a true exchange of value that improves the patient journey and clinical outcomes, and the healthcare worker's efficiency and work satisfaction. I believe it is a way of improving healthcare affordability, accessibility and availability that resonates with everyone.

MAIN POINTS:

1. Understand current trends to anticipate future ones
2. Healthcare cost pressures are increasing for multiple reasons
3. Replacing our disease-care mindset with a health-care mindset opens new possibilities
4. Social determinants of health are an under-utilised tool for improving healthcare
5. Improving the experience for patients and healthcare staff should be the focus of improvements, including technological

2 WHY IMPROVE HEALTHCARE?

> 'Sub-optimal care is the third highest cause of death in developed healthcare systems – and system problems, rather than mistakes, are the highest contributors.'
>
> **Martin Makary, M.D., M.P.H.**

While improving healthcare by restoring its 'heart' is the right thing to do, there is also the hard economic fact that countries around the world are struggling to afford equitable systems that provide healthcare that is available, affordable *and* accessible. Isolated improvements haven't resulted in dramatic healthcare system improvements[1-3].

Healthcare funding directly impacts other vital social programmes, such as education (Figure 2). Inadequate education and healthcare affect both current and future generations, with future costs and benefits directly attributable to current provision[4]. So how do we tackle the funding gap?

Despite the mainstream failure of health systems to cohesively grapple with effective healthcare delivery, the ideal trinity of great healthcare efficiency, fantastic outcomes, and high patient/ carer/worker satisfaction is possible. Effective healthcare is cheaper healthcare, because it is designed to benefit all involved - staff, patients and carers. This reduces costs because there is less waste, less rework and fewer errors with expensive rectification.

WHAT ABOUT ERRORS?

Only a fraction of medical injuries and litigation actually arise from negligence, or inadequate quality of care. Improved teamwork that enhances staff engagement and increases patient/staff/carer satisfaction reduces litigation more so than does quality of care. Effective healthcare is a proactive team sport, building long-term value for the patient (player), trainers (caregivers) and spectators (community). Compare this with the current system that is largely reactive and transactional - treating when ill - and ignores patients in between episodes of care[5-8].

As raised above, lapses in the safety and quality of healthcare have enormous financial costs for patients and the health system. They also take a toll on people's lives and social networks. The costs of these failures are underestimated, as they do not factor in the indirect healthcare and societal costs[9]. In Australia it is estimated that:

- Healthcare associated injury and ill health add 13–16% to hospital costs alone — or one in every seven dollars spent on hospital care[10, 11];
- There are approximately 190,000 medicine-related hospital admissions in Australia each year, with an estimated direct cost of A$660 million (US$429 million) and indirect costs of a similar magnitude[12];
- At current rates, the total estimated cost attributable to falls-related injury will increase almost threefold from A$498 million (US$323 million) per year in 2001 to A$1,375 million per year in 2051.3 (US$893 million)[13]; and
- Modelling estimates of excess length of stay (LOS)

attributed to surgical site infection (SSI) range between 3.5 and 23 days, depending on the type of infection. It is estimated that the total national number of hospital bed days lost to SSI for a one year period was 206,527, costing between A$250 million and $500 million per annum Encouragingly, systematic surveillance has shown reductions of 11% or more per annum in SSI's[14-17].

In the US, it is estimated that the third leading cause of death, after heart disease and cancer, is now preventable medical errors. This is higher than an older landmark Australian study, which may reflect technical medical advances out-pacing system improvements. A 2010 study released by the US Society of Actuaries estimated that medical errors cost the American economy at least US$19.5 billion. Of that, about US$17 billion was due to increased medical costs, US$1.1 billion to lost productivity from short-term disability claims, and US$1.4 billion from increased mortality rates. Error rates in developing countries are similar to those in developed countries (3-17%), however, the consequences are much higher – mortality is in the order of 30%, compared to 2-16% in developed countries[9, 14, 18].

So direct costs are attributable to suboptimal care, never mind the personal cost to patients, families, and carers. While a new budget can be handed down each year, a new body or life cannot. Patients have their entire lifespan to live or endure with the consequences of suboptimal care[18].

SUB-OPTIMAL CARE AND HAND-OVER

What is the high impact area to target to minimise this

problem? Clinical handover is a high-risk scenario for patient safety, and driver of unnecessary cost in both acute and chronic care. At its most innocuous, poor handover leads to duplicated work with wasted staff time and healthcare resources and a poor patient experience. At its worst, discontinuity of care leads to adverse events and litigation. Australian and US studies have found 11-15% of handovers are inadequate and lead to adverse events, compared to 6% of adverse events that are due to inadequate skill levels of practitioners.

Some numbers help to illustrate the importance of clinical handover:

- Over 30 million days of hospital care occur in Australia per annum, where in-hospital handover occurs three times per day with each nursing shift, once or more daily from medical care to nursing care (90+ million episodes);
- Over 10 million operations occur annually in Australia, with four or more handovers when passing from the ward to the operating room, recovery room and back to the ward (40+ million episodes); and
- An Australian coordination of healthcare study in 2016-2017 found that 17% of people saw three or more health professionals for the same condition. 12% of these reported that there were issues caused by a lack of communication between the health professionals. This was more common with older patients, and patients with long-term disease conditions, both growing sectors [19].

TRANSITIONS AND LONGITUDINAL CARE

US estimates are of 30% waste of expenditure in healthcare delivery, or around US$1 trillion per annum. The Organisation for Economic Cooperation and Development (OECD) estimates are of 20% wasted spend. Australian estimates are much 'better' at 15% - however this is still in the order of A$20 billion per annum. Imagine the benefit to society of making use of this wasted funding. Transitions of care provide multiple system intervention points [20-22]. So what is the solution? Where do we go from here?

Unfortunately, the current financial design of healthcare delivery in Australia and elsewhere reflects a transactional mindset. This financial design treats healthcare interventions as 'one-offs', ignoring the ongoing healthcare needs or context of the patient. The longitudinal or lifelong nature of healthcare delivery is not accounted for. This is mirrored in the major cost indicators for healthcare spending - the Pharmaceutical Benefits Scheme (PBS) and the Medical Benefits Schedule (MBS). These are usually labelled drivers of cost and are targeted as such for cost containment measures. In fact, they are lag indicators, telling us where the cost outcomes are occurring, and not where the drivers of those costs are [4].

In 2001, the United States Institute of Medicine issued a now famous report "Crossing the Quality Chasm." The report describes six outcome dimensions of high quality healthcare. In every dimension, the system was deemed to be underperforming, with people not getting the healthcare they deserved. Revision of this framework in recent years has emphasized Value, which is a ratio of quality and cost of care, and Equity. Equity, or access to care, is a problem throughout the world. There is also an emphasis on preventative care, not just acute care [23].

REDESIGN OUTCOMES:

1. **Safe:** avoiding injuries to patients from the care that is intended to help them.
2. **Effective:** providing services based on scientific knowledge to all who could benefit, and refraining from providing services to those not likely to benefit.
3. **Patient-centered:** providing care that is respectful of and responsive to individual patient preferences, needs, and values, and ensuring that patient values guide all clinical decisions.
4. **Timely:** reducing waits and sometimes harmful delays for both those who receive and those who give care.
5. **Efficient:** avoiding waste, including waste of effort, equipment, supplies, ideas, and energy.
6. **Equitable:** providing care that does not vary in quality because of personal characteristics such as gender, ethnicity, geographic location, and socioeconomic status.

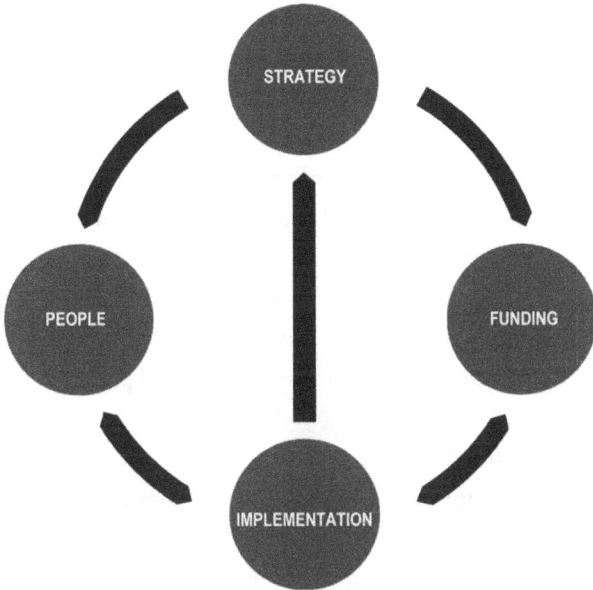

FIGURE 4   Changing Healthcare

PRACTICAL MODELS

These outcome measures led the International Consortium for Health Outcomes Measures (ICHOM) to develop tools to measure outcomes that matter to patients. Knowing what matters to patients, the recipients of care, enables targeted improvements to healthcare delivery - improvements that matter. Improvements can target the following outcomes (Figure 4):

1. **Implementation**
    - Reengineering care processes from the user's perspective
    - Effective use of information technologies

- Coordination of care across patient-conditions, services, sites of care and time
2. **People**
   - Knowledge and skills management
   - Development of effective teams
   - Accessible, available and affordable care
3. **Strategy**
   - A shift from reactive, disease-treatment to proactive health optimisation
   - Designing care around people and patients, not institutions
4. **Funding**
   - A move from volume-based reward, to value-based reward
   - Improving clinical outcomes alongside business outcomes

VOLUME VERSUS VALUE-BASED CARE

With the current use of 'lag' indicators, PBS cost containment via supplier negotiation and supply chain efficiencies is expected to save A$6.6 billion per annum However, this is only one part of the system. To use outcome measures, effort should be applied to ensuring appropriate use, or to matching the cost of usage against the outcome cost of different medications, including no treatment. An example is the use of anti-nausea medications, where the more expensive items are more effective and reduce other costs such as staff-time managing a sick patient, and consumables required for cleaning up. Isolated cost-containment of medication usage here drives up other costs that outweigh the savings generated. As importantly, the patient experience is impaired, leading to poorer clinical outcomes for the same technical result.

MBS cost-containment measures include innovations around delivery of primary care, complex and chronic care, and aged care. This makes sense when we see doctor visits are high compared to our peer countries, and in light of knowing the costs created by inadequate transitions of patient care. This approach targets, at most, 60% of the healthcare spend. The other 40% of health spend is on hospital services, and no coordinated approach exists to measure their indirect costs and target these – or to derive synergies from one system to the other [1, 4, 11, 24].

In the 2016-2017 year, 13% of the population were admitted to hospital. There were 173 hospital discharges per 1,000 population in Australia in 2016, which is at the higher end of international comparisons, with Germany 252, USA 125 and Canada 83 per 1,000 population. Repeat admissions account for a higher ratio of discharges (17%) than population admitted. Recent measures to reduce readmissions in cardiac and diabetic patients have proven successful on clinical, financial and patient experience measures [11, 25].

Targeting indirect costs such as treatment delays, duplicated effort and wasted materials is all the more important when we consider that despite hospital length of stay being amongst the lowest in the world, healthcare costs in Australia are middling. Average days to discharge in 2015 for Australia was 4.8, USA 5.4 and Canada 7.6 days, without significant cost-shifting to other parts of the healthcare system. Reducing bed-days further is unlikely. We must therefore focus our efforts on other parts of the treatment chain, such as workflows and the user experience, to further drive down healthcare costs [11].

Healthcare leaders and professionals are being asked to focus on quality and patient safety in ways they never have before, because the economics of quality are changing. Fortunately, quality care is less expensive care, because a better patient and staff experience occurs through a more efficient, less wasteful process, with fewer mistakes and less patient harm or injury. Unnecessarily high personal and societal financial costs are incurred when quality care is not delivered consistently throughout the healthcare system. As shown above, we can, and need, to use the business machinery of healthcare delivery to foster and support quality of care, rather than relying exclusively on clinical measures to deliver these outcomes.

MAIN POINTS:

1. Healthcare funding has current and future effects on society
2. Sub-optimal healthcare has human and financial costs. Errors are a small part
3. Healthcare handover is a vital, over-looked component of quality, cost-effective care
4. Redesign principles for healthcare delivery that include 'What matters to patients' ensure relevance for staff and patients
5. Both business and clinical measures impact value delivery in healthcare

3 WHY DO I WANT TO IMPROVE HEALTHCARE?

'Simple can be harder than complex: You have to work hard to get your thinking clean to make it simple. But it's worth it in the end because once you get there, you can move mountains.'

Steve Jobs, Apple

A call to arms is met with familiar cries. 'It's just the way healthcare is.' Believing that the earth is flat doesn't make it true, and the same goes for the belief that we can't improve healthcare. 'It's too complex.' Of this there is no doubt. Like a hydra, its many heads act independently. Even worse, in the same way the mythological monster grew two new heads if one was removed, healthcare appears to become more complex in response to 'improvement measures'. So, how do we improve healthcare? I believe that improvement measures alone are not what is needed. In my view, a complete redesign is required.

I've always loved reducing complexity, whether to improve understanding, get the job done more easily or safely, speed things up or improve outcomes. When confronted with a problem I try to cherry pick and apply the best solutions available, from any industry anywhere in the world. This ensures success is more likely - not just 'satisfactory' success - *great success*.

ON DIAGNOSIS

The difficulty in healthcare lies in diagnosing problems correctly. Often, multiple and diverse symptoms relate to one common problem, rather than multiple problems. This helps explain why multiple improvement measures often don't yield the expected results. In medical school we were encouraged to apply Occam's (or Ockhams's) razor to diagnosis. Rather than attributing each symptom a patient had to a different disease, we were taught to select the one disease that included the greatest number of symptoms.

It is a common shortcoming in healthcare to consider a symptom in isolation and to create an entirely logical 'solution' to this symptom. If it is not the underlying problem, it is destined to fail. We often see this in healthcare IT solutions, which contain logical independent steps that become unworkable in the dynamic setting of healthcare delivery. Many large-scale healthcare delivery programmes struggle from an incomplete consideration of context – the individual patient or user, their interactions with others, the long-term nature of patients' lives, and staff and patient affiliations with healthcare institutions. 60-70% of change projects fail to meet all three objectives of on time, on budget and within scope [1].

DOCTORS VS MANAGEMENT

I didn't start out being interested in healthcare management. As a medical student and a young doctor in the late 1980's and early 1990's, my focus was very much on the academic. Management was something intermittently interacted with, usually for a specific purpose, such as obtaining leave or ensuring overtime was paid. No teaching was supplied to explain that optimising the business side of healthcare could be used as a tool to improve clinical outcomes, by enabling resources to be made available for clinical healthcare instead of being consumed administratively. The closest case studies to this concept were public health measures, and preventative health programmes. However, these were, and still are, couched in terms of delivering clinical care, and ignore the health benefits of optimising care delivery in a business sense, in order that healthcare can be more available, accessible and affordable. Efficiency, engagement and empowerment are all tools to further improve the health of individuals and the population.

Conversely, the absence of administrators and management on wards and in emergency departments, and the resultant lack of interaction with clinical staff, sent a message that there was indifference and poor understanding of the clinical world. Even now, a common model is to leave the clinical work to clinicians, and the business work to administrators. This inevitably results in uncoordinated bursts of activity and an 'us-and-them' mentality, creating cultural barriers to change. These barriers include a lack of openness and trust, and the withholding of information.

BENEFITS OF BUREAUCRACY

The effects of an us-and-them culture really crystallised for me in the mid-1990's. I spent a couple of years as a medical officer with the Australian Defence Force. This was the first time in my life that I was required to interact with a large administrative infrastructure in conjunction with the treatment of patients.

Dealing with patients in the Defence Force entailed dealing with their administrative unit at the same time. The context of the patient became essential in this setting, as these patients were integral and vital components of functional teams. If one team member was unwell, a plane or warship might not be able to depart its base. A substitute could often not readily be found without compromising the capability of another team or unit. A comparable situation occurs in civilian life with airlines - and also with operating theatre teams.

This made me more aware of how important a patient's context is to their clinical condition. Optimising clinical outcomes required consideration of contextual factors outside my medically trained expertise. Knowing 'the system', and hence the multiple ways possible of achieving a desired outcome, were essential. This meant that non-clinical knowledge could be as important as clinical knowledge in optimising a patient's outcome.

DRAWBACKS OF BUREAUCRACY

On my return to civilian life my focus returned to studying for my anaesthesia specialisation in the late 1990s. Management was seen as a necessary evil supporting the infrastructure and logistics for treating patients, and sometimes interfering with the process. There seemed to be a slow increase in the numbers of people in administration roles with a slow dilution of those with direct hands-on exposure to patients. This trend has been particularly pronounced in the US, as graphically demonstrated in Figure 5. Increases in the cost of healthcare delivery have trended with increases in the administrative burden, far outstripping inflation and consumer price indices. While these figures come from America, the Australian experience is similar.

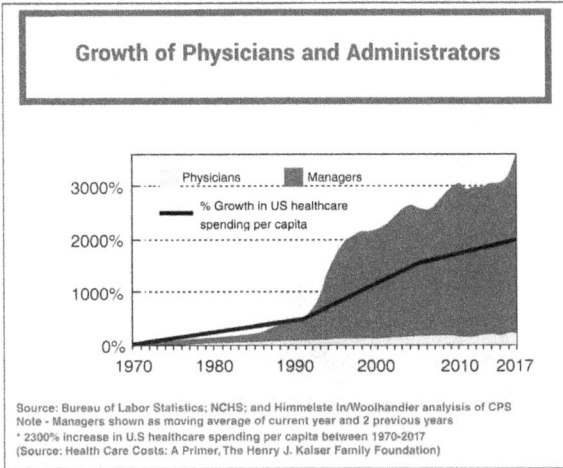

Growth of Physicians and Administrators

Physicians | Managers
% Growth in US healthcare spending per capita

3000%
2000%
1000%
0%

1970 1980 1990 2000 2010 2017

Source: Bureau of Labor Statistics; NCHS; and Himmelste ln/Woolhandler analyisis of CPS
Note - Managers shown as moving average of current year and 2 previous years
* 2300% increase in U.S healthcare spending per capita between 1970-2017
(Source: Health Care Costs: A Primer, The Henry J. Kaiser Family Foundation)

FIGURE 5   Growth of Clinicians and Administrators

'It is amazing that people who think we cannot afford to pay for doctors, hospitals and medication, somehow think that we can afford to pay for doctors, hospitals, medication and a government bureaucracy to administer it.'

Thomas Sowell

At the time, I noticed that clinicians and administrators often worked at cross-purposes, even though they were both providing for patients. Doctors may intuitively understand when a treatment is superior, whether due to a shorter recovery, less resource-intensive treatment or an earlier return to work. This saves the individual and the community money, both directly and indirectly, through increased productivity.

THE SYSTEM

However, there is no system to track these expenses and benefits in order to demonstrate that value. Consequently, an administrator may see higher direct costs without being able to see the reduced indirect costs. For the episode of care there may be an overall cost saving; however, it is not necessarily visible. The administrator's logical conclusion will be that the more expensive treatment merely costs more money for no discernible benefit. Measures are taken in error to 'rein in costs' on the visible item, generating increased costs on unmeasured items. Fortunately, technology can now be used to inexpensively create insights where it has previously not appeared cost-effective to do so. To paraphrase Drucker 'What gets measured gets improved' [2].

Alternatively, there is the 'wrong pockets' problem, where a superior episode of care may cost one healthcare provider more, so they avoid it, even though it saves another healthcare provider and/or the community money overall. By evaluating and funding pilot programmes and enabling the commercialisation of proven programmes, this problem can be tackled [3].

Worse than this, one treatment may earn a provider a higher margin, independent of its benefit to the individual and/ or the community. This moral hazard can lead to healthcare enterprises becoming optimised for revenue generation, rather than healthcare value. This applies, to varying degrees, whatever the healthcare delivery system.

Healthcare delivery in many countries is provided by both the government and the non-government ('private') sector. For both government and non-government enterprises that deliver products and services, the aims are to deliver the highest quality, at the lowest cost, and with the best experience for the consumer. The most successful organisations do more than one of these things at the same time. Clinical care has tended to focus on *quality*, with less regard for the other factors. Healthcare administration has tended to focus on *cost*, with less regard for the other factors. Much gets lost in translation, resulting in a suboptimal system.

GOOD BUSINESS

This was the motivation to start a management qualification - a desire to speak the language of business and government, to better articulate the value of quality healthcare. Through this study I was delighted to discover that good business values the consumer as an individual. It takes time to discover their problems and create solutions for them. Good business doesn't 'trick' the consumer into purchasing a product. 'Good' businesses prosper through good times and bad because they deliver value to the consumer. There are similarities in delivering good healthcare to patients – taking time to discover your patient's problems, provide solutions and help them to choose and implement a solution appropriate to them. The longer-term benefit to the patient and community is a more productive individual, with less time lost to ill health.

In contrast to this, 'bad' businesses might convince consumers that they require products or services that they don't need. This was particularly the case from the 1960s to the 1980s, when the simplest way to increase sales was to increase the advertising budget. Consumers had no readily obtainable alternative means of information and relied on the sources available to them –

print and television media. Without readily available alternative information an asymmetric supply of information led individuals to predictable conclusions and purchasing decisions. This, and the commercial exploitation of hospitals in Australia at around the same time (*see* Introduction), helps to explain the medical community's distaste, aversion to, and mistrust of commercial enterprises, that has led to a disregard of business processes as another means of achieving clinical outcomes.

A TURNING POINT

I made use of my business studies in pro bono work with hospitals, the Australian Medical Association and the Australian Society of Anaesthetists. Life was comfortable, professionally and personally. In my early forties I felt well. I kept an eye on my blood pressure and exercised regularly, at a gym during the week and cycling with mates at the weekend. Then the event occurred that crystallised the importance of my observations of the shortcomings of the healthcare system. I became a patient. Not just any patient - a cancer patient.

In hindsight, I had several months of intermittent abdominal sensations that seemed to improve with a change in diet - avoiding dairy products, and using probiotics. Then blood in a bowel motion occurred and was dutifully checked out. I was unexpectedly diagnosed with bowel cancer, with no risk factors. This wasn't in my life plan. My grandmother lived until she was 103. That was my life plan.

Along with the 'loss' of my expected future, I gained a ringside seat to being a patient. Not an elective patient with a first world problem – one with a life-threatening illness. Despite knowing beforehand that this was a small possibility amongst other more likely diagnoses, it was a major shock to have to face this fact. I assumed it would be caught early. What I wasn't prepared for were investigations on lungs and brain to check for any cancer spread, and being booked for a major operation - a bowel resection - the next week. Suddenly I was no longer in control. This wasn't supposed to happen to doctors.

Lying alone in my hospital room, I began to muse on healthcare's heart - where had it gone? When staff actually care it makes a massive difference. Not just to help the patient through the day, but to actual healthcare outcomes. Wouldn't it be great if there was a system to help improve the experience of healthcare, as well as reduce its risk and cost? A better healthcare experience, not just for patients, but for staff and doctors as well [4].

DISCONNECTED

The dislocation and dysfunction of the healthcare system was highlighted for me during this treatment. Each stage of the process felt disconnected from the next. The experience when moving between community care and hospital care, or between different areas within the hospital, was impaired by repetition as a compliance requirement, rather than repeated checks for the purpose of improving the patient experience. Significantly, this also impairs the experience for the healthcare provider - it breeds frustration and a sense of loss of control. Performing functions purely to meet external requirements brings a disconnect between the process and its outcome [5].

As a patient, I finished up feeling like a collection of parts or experiences that didn't quite mesh, instead of having different perspectives of the same experience. This sensation of being a component that doesn't quite fit into a larger process is similar to the sense of not belonging to a team that is often experienced by healthcare workers. The consequences are: reduced engagement; reduced efficiency; increased waste and risk; and disempowerment, with an impaired experience for both healthcare provider and patient. The loss of purpose in work is an important outcome of this disconnect, leading to burnout, career changes or worse [5].

By applying Occam's Razor, the solution then is to *start* with the healthcare experience. This is the common factor which is impaired for clinicians, administrators and patients. By improving the user experience we create value in healthcare for all participants, and generate the improvements in quality and cost that are essential for healthcare's effective delivery. We also position the industry to adapt to and take advantage of the innovations in service delivery that we see in other industries - and that are yet to come.

MAIN POINTS:

1. Healthcare is getting more complex
2. We need better healthcare system diagnoses
3. Management and clinician collaboration benefits patients – and improves the experience for patients, staff and clinicians
4. Good business (healthcare) looks after customers (patients)
5. The user experience integrates the clinical and business worlds

4 TOP ISSUES CONFRONTING HEALTHCARE

'We build our business systems the way we build our cities:
over time, without a plan, on top of ruins.'

Gene Brown

The problems and challenges faced by the vast majority of healthcare organisations are remarkably similar. They stem from an industry undergoing widespread change, enabled by technology, and driven by the expectations of patients, staff and doctors. I believe that we are seeing a shift from episodic, reactive treatment of disease to large scale, proactive optimisation of health. However, without coordinated improvement measures, this is putting the healthcare system under strain, and patients, staff and doctors are suffering as a result. Healthcare is losing its heart, and becoming cold [1].

When meeting with senior clinical and administrative decision-makers in both my healthcare consultancy role and in my role as a specialist anaesthetist, I analyse healthcare problems with the expertise of business and clinical training and experience, *and* a patient perspective from my cancer surgery. I believe that healthcare complexity has increased beyond the ability of any one individual to ensure excellence in all aspects of care. In the same way that a collaborative team oversees the building of a skyscraper, rather than the responsibility falling to an individual builder, we now require collaborative teams to lead healthcare organisations, and to deliver care for individuals [2].

All industries have seen the loss of the generalist and the rise of the specialist, as have all healthcare disciplines – both clinical and managerial. This change is driven by the explosion of knowledge, such that individuals 'know more and more about less and less'. As well, consumers want healthcare experts who know a lot about a small area, not someone who knows a little about a wide range of things. The best healthcare teams therefore combine a range of health disciplines to ensure that value is delivered by and for the healthcare system. They bridge the gap between the business side and the clinical side of healthcare delivery and unlock engagement, efficiency and empowerment.

MAIN ISSUES FACING HOSPITALS

The hospitals that I work with are community-based and non-governmental, and undertake a wide range of surgeries. Many are stand-alone facilities; some are part of state- or national-networks. The sorts of issues that I see are:

Operational issues – these tend to dominate people's daily work, and include:

1. Ensuring appropriate resourcing for routine and unexpected requirements, in the face of increased patient and treatment complexities;
2. Reducing resource and energy usage;

3. Security of information, people and equipment;
4. 'Leapfrog' development such as moving from paper to computerised systems, or adding a new department; and
5. Optimising C-suite to employee communication: avoiding information loss, and translating the vision for the enterprise to daily tasks.

People issues – these relate to administrative and nurse employees, patients, and visiting clinical staff, and include:

1. Attracting and retaining top-quality people;
2. Reducing the use of 'temporary' staff, with associated higher costs and reduced efficiency;
3. 'Presentee-ism' - pleasant under-performance, instead of the required engagement and efficiency;
4. Ensuring that the healthcare experience meets patient, carer, staff and clinician expectations; and
5. Creating value for relationships with community doctors.

Financial issues - these exert pressure on decision-making, with the moral hazard and 'wrong pocket' effects described in the previous chapter [3, 4]. Symptoms include:

1. Payroll costs, a healthcare enterprise's major outlay;
2. Clinical variances and cost outliers, where treatments and/ or clinicians' costs-incurred exceed benchmarks;
3. A reduction in revenue streams from macro-economic pressures, competition and fewer customers holding private health insurance;
4. Pricing/cost transparency, in particular for medications, devices and insurances; and
5. Reducing margins.

Strategic issues – these tend to be drowned out by day-to-day operations, with a culture of putting out operational fires [5-10]. Issues include:

1. Modernisation: ways to consistently assess the next "big thing" whether it is equipment, medications, operations, technology or new healthcare delivery models;
2. Competition from similar and/or alternative healthcare providers;
3. Governance: meeting external compliance requirements alongside continuous regulatory/legislative change;
4. Risk: improving the safety/quality culture to reduce business *and* clinical errors; and
5. How to improve collaboration with patients, staff, and clinicians, to ensure mutual benefit.

These issues are found worldwide. In its annual survey, the American College of Healthcare Executives (ACHE) asked respondents to rank ten issues affecting their hospitals in order of how pressing they were, and to identify specific areas of concern within each of those issues. Financial challenges ranked number one on the list of hospital CEOs' top concerns. Patient safety and quality ranked second, followed by complying with government mandates [11].

"While financial challenges remain the top concern for CEOs, survey results suggest that senior leaders still have their eye on their organization's financial strategy, and they are also making strides in moving forward patient safety and quality initiatives," says Deborah J. Bowen, FACHE, CAE, president and CEO of ACHE. The rise in importance of personnel shortages, from the 10th-ranked problem in 2015 to more recently a fourth-ranked issue indicates organisations are concerned about recruiting and retaining the right talent, and recognise the link between top talent and reduced operational risk and cost.

The survey was sent to 1,054 community hospital CEOs, of whom 350 (33 percent) responded. These are non-federal, short-term admission, non-specialty hospitals - which is the niche that I target in Australia. While the issues listed by survey respondents are of pressing concern to them, they do not necessarily reflect their hospital's current priorities. Ideally, managing these pressing issues would simultaneously progress and support hospital priorities.

MATCHING STRATEGY TO THE FRONT-LINE

For example, addressing concerns with a user experience improvement programme creates new opportunities to incorporate ongoing hospital priorities, such as compliance reporting. Recall that improving the user experience is a potent differentiator for attracting and retaining top talent, whether it is visiting medical specialists, employees, and even preferred patients. Improving the user experience ensures improvement programmes gain traction, and, as importantly, persist [12].

Patient safety and quality of care is of particular concern. Healthcare associated injury adds **13%-16%** to hospital costs per annum [13, 14].

Causes include:

1. **Surgical site infection** is estimated to cost over 200,000 bed days per annum, in the order of A$200 million per annum;

2. **Falls-related costs** were A$498 million per annum in 2001 and on current trends are projected to rise to A$1,375 million in 2051;

3. **Clinical handover** is a potent time of risk: up to 50% of information is lost, *whether handed over or not* [15, 16]; and

4. **Medication safety:** there are ~190,000 medicine-related hospital admissions each year in Australia, at a cost of A$660 million per annum.

The Australian Commission on Safety and Quality in Healthcare identifies the following factors as priorities for healthcare organisations to reduce healthcare risk and cost [13]:

1. Optimal antimicrobial use and containment of resistance would allow A$300 million to be saved/redirected;

2. Recognising/responding to patient deterioration permits earlier intervention with faster recovery, lower financial cost to healthcare, and less personal cost to the patient;

3. Developing a positive safety culture that addresses the potential for mishap, rather than responding to mishaps [17];

4. Supporting implementation of improvement initiatives through preplanning, focusing on the patient, and adapting to context (functional unit, hospital, health system); and

5. Supporting safety with (and despite) e-health.

WHAT ARE THE DRIVERS?

We know that rising healthcare costs are not sustainable. All 'westernised' systems are grappling with this problem. Paradoxically, commercial insurers have conflicting incentives on healthcare costs. To some degree, their profit is a margin on top of their costs, meaning that a higher turnover can return a higher profit. Similarly, 'big pharma' and prosthetic suppliers have the same pricing paradox, and volume-based healthcare rebates don't provide any incentive to rein in healthcare costs [18].

In fact, the rebate system probably indirectly and unintentionally provides incentive to generate costs. To paraphrase Ducker, a father of management science, our current healthcare system is perfectly designed to get the results it gets. Reward is proportional to the volume of care delivered, not to the value to the individual or the community – hence volume or throughput is maximised. The system needs to be redesigned to reward the value provided to patients and society [19].

We know healthcare needs to be cheaper and safer, and that the user experience needs to be better for patients and providers. This 'disruption' will expand accessibility of healthcare to where and when it is required, rather than restricting it according to health funders' budgets and health providers' work practices. Many needs, including unmet ones, can be covered primarily by technology, enabling access wherever and whenever the patient requires. Covering high volume requirements, especially of a routine nature, is where technology really adds value.

Humans add value to 'non-routine' healthcare, where creativity and human interaction are of great importance. If we imagine healthcare delivery as a pyramid, technology delivers the base, humans the peak, and a combination of the two makes up the centre – refer to Figure 6. In this way, everybody wins - healthcare availability and accessibility increase, average costs go down, and humans are more engaged in the interesting cases.

An added benefit is an increase of meaning in work, improving engagement, efficiency and empowerment, and tackling mid-career burnout.

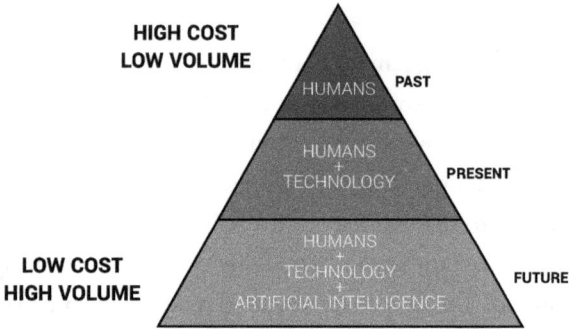

FIGURE 6   Future Healthcare Delivery

To see some examples of how technology can deliver healthcare, refer to www.healthtap.com (US) and www.babylonhealth.com (UK) which go far beyond telemedicine by using decision support and pattern recognition algorithms to provide tailored recommendations without human intervention. To understand the scale of this service delivery, 108,000 doctors are registered with HealthTap, 6.8 billion answers have been served and 24,810 lives have been saved (company data as at 24 DEC 2017). Delivering such a resource around the clock with our traditional service delivery model is not possible [20].

Personalised human advice can subsequently be obtained via the above portals, where both patient and healthcare provider are pre-screened to provide a match for the patient and likely condition. www.onemedical.com is another example of a hybrid technology-human model that enables more patient-provider time.

Disruption is occurring to the current disease-care delivery model. Instead of delivering care primarily in response to disease - which implies the 1% of the population which is unwell - healthcare can also be delivered proactively to the 99% of the population who are currently well - 'pre-patients'. Using technology, this 'wellness delivery' can reach vast audiences cheaply and readily, much like social media. In this way, the 'disruption' of healthcare delivery is constructive, as it will increase inexpensively preventative healthcare for the well, and 'worried well', while freeing up human-intensive resources for the treatment of patients who are actually unwell [21].

MAIN POINTS:

1. Widespread change is stressing healthcare and its people
2. Issues facing hospitals are found worldwide
3. Healthcare complexity means we need teams
4. Matching strategic needs with front-line needs is problematic
5. Changing incentives and harnessing technology will help

5 HUMAN OUTCOMES OF PROBLEMS

'A bad system will beat a good person every time'.

W. Edwards Deming

As the preceding chapter demonstrates, it is much easier to highlight problems than to propose solutions. And if solutions are proposed, they tend to be on a micro, rather than a macro, level. What is the 'glue' that can tie disparate solutions together? We need to think in terms of the healthcare system as a whole, not in terms of isolated improvements without consideration of upstream and downstream effects. How can thinking in systems work in practice to improve healthcare accessibility, affordability and availability?

During impressive advances in technology, medication, equipment and knowledge over the last few decades, one aspect of healthcare has been very much overlooked - the human experience. This parallels a rise in dissatisfaction with healthcare over the last few decades. We see usage rates of 40% for complementary and alternative medicine (CAM) in Australia and the USA [1, 2], and demands from patients to have more control over their healthcare information and choices. It is no accident that improving the healthcare experience is my number one fix.

THE UNSPOKEN EPIDEMIC

The other side of this dissatisfaction is the high rate of healthcare worker burnout. This is a serious problem. Over half of Australian and US clinicians are experiencing symptoms of burnout – up to two times that of the general population, and up to three times the rate for other professionals [3, 4]. Similarly, 32% of nurses in Australia are considering leaving the profession, at a time when the shortfall of nurses is increasing [5]. If burnout was an infection, there would be a worldwide response to this epidemic.

Burnout syndrome is characterised by emotional exhaustion (losing enthusiasm for work) and depersonalisation (treating people as if they were objects). Burnout results in reduced professional effort, with implications for reduced productivity and increased errors. It can lead to early retirement, or career change, and can contribute to absolute workforce shortages (inadequate national supply) and relative workforce shortages (inadequate regional availability of numbers and/or types of clinician). It also contributes to an increased risk of suicide [4-6].

The primary drivers of burnout, and conversely of satisfaction, among clinicians are seen in Figure 7 [6]:

1.   Workload,
2.   Efficiency,
3.   Autonomy in work,
4.   Work-life integration, and
5.   Meaning in work.

These drivers in turn are affected by four main factors: individual characteristics, work unit dynamics, organisational culture and national requirements/trends. At first glance it appears difficult to reconcile these competing demands.

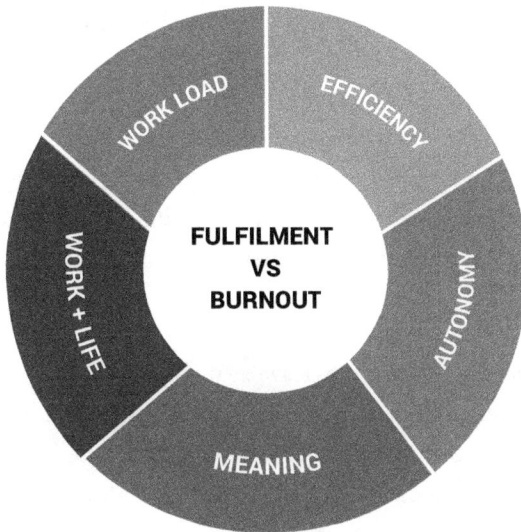

FIGURE 7   Burnout

Workload is poorly related to volume of work - it depends on factors such as practice location, workplace design and ergonomics; speciality and team structure, compensation arrangements, personal financial pressures, and compliance requirements. The impact of one extra case differs enormously for each speciality. A simple example is the length of a typical eye procedure (15-20 minutes) compared to a neurosurgical operation (2-4 hours). Financial pressures may result in increased workload, as a way of increasing revenue.

Efficiency is affected by training and experience, processes, team composition, integration of care and compliance requirements.

The services offered by a particular hospital vary with size and location, affecting team composition and integration of care. Some sites naturally attract individuals with particular interests, who more readily form self-supporting teams that promote engagement and efficiency.

Autonomy varies with personality, control of scheduling, care guidelines, referral patterns and reimbursement restrictions. Again, different geographic locations and hospital sizes place more (or less) onerous requirements on individuals.

Work-life integration depends on personal values and those of dependents, scheduling, leave availability and provision, and certification requirements. Often we have little control over the external macro-factors. However, insufficient attention is often paid to accommodating individual needs as a way of decreasing the impact of external factors.

Meaning in work is affected by self-awareness of purpose and of achievements, ability to shape career, professional and patient relationships, opportunities for learning and development, organisational purpose, culture and values, and the impact of national priorities on healthcare. Again, while we may have little control over the macro-factors, insufficient attention is paid to individual needs and wants.

Tragically, burnout can lead to suicide. For any individual to feel under such pressure that taking their own life seems like the only option is in itself a tragedy. The ripple effect is also significant. There are lifelong repercussions for those around the deceased, impacting on quality of life for loved ones left behind. There is also a correlation with a higher risk of suicide for those left behind at personal, work unit and institutional levels, whether they personally knew the deceased or not [7]. From a purely pragmatic point of view, society invests in people to train as healthcare workers, and to lose them from their career is a loss of that investment.

GENERIC FRAMEWORKS, INDIVIDUAL WORKPLACES

The complexity of healthcare delivery and enormous variation in size of facilities and mix of operations that they perform means that a 'one size fits all' approach to improving the user experience, healthcare quality and efficiency of delivery is doomed to fail. Therefore, an approach is required that minimises overlooking the essential elements, while allowing a degree of freedom for adaptation at the local level.

This was elegantly explained by the New York surgeon Atul Gawande [8], when refining the 'surgical checklist' to maximise its success at the local level. The reason or purpose for the checklist is emphasised – preventing wrong site/wrong surgery errors. As discussed elsewhere, this meaning or purpose in work is very motivating [9], and an essential part of any change programme. Secondarily, allowing individual teams to work out their details when implementing a change programme improves uptake and acceptance. The team then 'owns' the change, improving persistence of the change.

We cannot consider the needs of healthcare providers without considering the needs of patients, and the supporting role of management and administrative personnel to both groups.

Analysing problems from the perspective of the three groups (patients, healthcare providers and administration) makes any list of requirements very long. This further complicates the above preliminary analysis.

WHERE IS THE COMMON GROUND?

However, analysing problems from these different perspectives uncovers common ground, much of which is previously un-discovered and/or unacknowledged. For example, individuals in separate functional areas often unintentionally duplicate problem-solving efforts, on behalf of their patients or downstream staff. Awareness of this shared effort is the beginnings of shared purpose. Identifying a simplified workflow that reduces exertion for the participants provides early rewards. This encourages buy-in to the process [9].

In this way, problem-solving approaches (such as those at reference [10]) can address concerns of groups and individuals at a local level, while meeting requirements at national and institutional levels. A key component of a successful improvement initiative is a workshop. Workshops identify individual and local problems that are at the forefront to those affected. They also promote engagement and empowerment at individual and team levels, which leads to efficiency improvements through the team-building that results.

Linking the solving of local problems with organisational purpose and improvement projects translates abstract organisational initiatives to the concrete local level. This improves healthcare provider satisfaction, reduces burnout and errors, and improves efficiency. It also improves the patient experience which improves clinical outcomes and referrals. So by thinking in systems we tackle healthcare's biggest hidden problems, user interactions, and find our greatest opportunities to reduce healthcare's biggest known problems.

MAIN POINTS:

1. The healthcare system is making us unwell
2. Burnout is a healthcare workforce crisis
3. We need individualised workplaces
4. Consider patients, staff and clinicians to find common ground
5. Link common ground to organisational objectives

6 HEALTHCARE SYSTEM MISTAKES

'94% of all failure is a result of the system... not people.'

W. Edwards Deming

In the last chapter, we looked at the downsides of our current 'healthcare system' on patients, staff and doctors. Improvement in healthcare delivery requires thinking about how to systematically understand its problems. These problems are not just isolated, episodic errors in healthcare delivery. There are also errors in long-term healthcare delivery – spending time and money with no long-term benefit to the patient or community, or saving money now that costs the community and patient more over the course of a patient's lifetime, through lost productivity or quality of life.

While errors are uncommon in healthcare, they are not rare. Individually, we may only see an error every year or so. No one would deny that this is uncommon. However, if we compare healthcare to other high-risk industries, we find that errors are far higher than they need to be. In particular, system errors are a part of the culture – 'that's the way it's always been' – and hence have become invisible; the elephant in the room. This contributes to the 20% (or more) waste in healthcare spending that is seen worldwide [1-4].

SYTEMIC WASTE

Why is this waste ingrained in healthcare, when other industries systematically root it out? One important reason is that usually very few individuals are affected in each healthcare system error, with relatively small individual expense. Collectively, these multiple small problems generate massive expense to society; however, the cost is diffused widely. Contrast this with a high-risk industry such as oil and gas, where a small mistake tends to create a large-scale disaster with many casualties, and a highly visible environmental impact.

With this in mind, Hudson analysed high-risk industries such as commercial aviation, the oil and gas industry, motor racing and the healthcare sector. He found that the exemplary safety records of other high-risk industries contrast with a much higher level of accidents in healthcare [5]. Why is this? The other industries mentioned had very poor safety records when they began. Contemporaneous newspapers are full of articles detailing the deaths of pilots and passengers, drivers and spectators, and miners.

ORGANISATIONAL ATTITUDE

Reasons for the present-day differences in error rates in different industries included organisational attitude and systemic management of risks. Different industries have matured at different rates in terms of attitude to risk and errors. Hudson describes organisational attitude in terms of having five stages of increasing trust and awareness around risk and error. These stages, as we move from Low- to High- Reliability Organisations, are (refer to Figure 8):

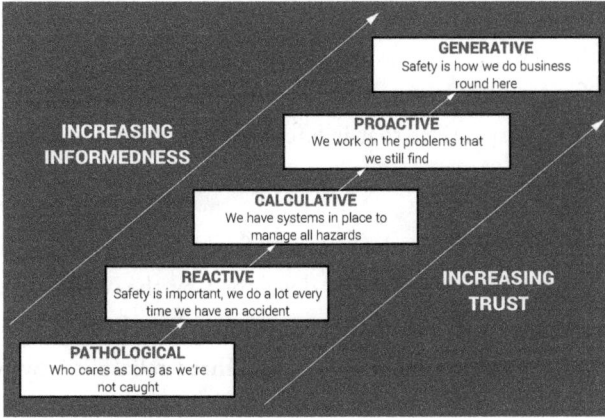

FIGURE 8   Hudson's Levels of Reliability

With respect to healthcare, a common flaw in thinking is that mistakes, while infrequent, are inevitable. At the start of my career mistakes were regarded commonly as 'one-offs', with the incorrect assumption that 'they won't happen again, so don't worry about it'. Sound familiar?

At an early stage in my specialist training, safety was regarded as important and a lot would get done every time there was a problem. This is a reactive, relatively immature 'Stage Two' organisational attitude to risk and error, being one step removed from regarding mistakes as 'one-offs'.

EXAMPLES IN HEALTHCARE

Currently, most of healthcare has systems in place to manage hazards – 'Stage Three' reliability. Champions of this revolution have been individuals such as the New York surgeon Gawande, organisations such as the Institute for Healthcare Improvement, the World Health Organisation, and the International Society for Quality in Healthcare. Gawande's book *The Checklist Manifesto* makes interesting reading for the personal and historical perspectives that it offers as healthcare has improved its reliability [6].

Of particular note is the Surgical Safety Checklist or Team Time Out (TTO) procedure developed by the World Health Organisation [7]. TTO and other measures have helped to move healthcare to this Calculative Stage Three reliability. Systems such as TTO are often criticised for interrupting workflows and being 'another piece of paper'. This is why it is important that methods for implementation are not prescribed - it is essential to allow local adaptation of safety measures to minimise disruption of existing workflows. This is critical for acceptance, adoption and ongoing adherence.

Increasingly, healthcare facilities, especially hospitals, are rolling out 'hazard reporting' systems to record near-misses (where there is no adverse outcome), in order to understand their frequency and how to systemise against repeat episodes. This is a Proactive 'Stage Four' reliability system, and is to be commended.

ORGANISATIONAL RISK

Other high-risk industries evolved in their attitudes to safety in a similar way – they didn't start 'safe'. When aviation began over 100 years ago it was a 'frontier occupation' where bravado was required. However, mistakes were almost always disastrous. Commercial aviation mistakes in particular lead to high visibility, high impact accidents with high personal, commercial and political costs. The resulting alignment of social, commercial and political awareness has meant that aviation safety was taken seriously from an early stage. Consequently, it is statistically more dangerous getting to and from the airport by car, than it is to fly [5]. Aviation transitioned from a 'Pathological' culture (Stage One) to a 'Generative' one (Stage Five), to use Hudson's stages, in a matter of decades.

Construction is also discussed in detail in Gawande's book, and compared and contrasted with healthcare. Similar safety issues arise in mega-projects, projects that span time-zones, cultures, decades and billions of dollars [8]. Problems in construction and mega-projects have high social, commercial and legal costs and, in order to deal with this complexity, the construction industry moved through the Calculative stage to Proactive and increasingly Generative stages of reliability some decades ago. So why is healthcare lagging?

Rishi Manchanda, MD, MPH, Founder of HealthBegins, tells a parable in an IHI Open School video short. Three friends come to a river filled with people being swept helplessly towards a waterfall. The first friend jumps in and frantically tries to save people who are just about to drown. *This sounds like healthcare workers at the coalface.* In an effort to improve the rescue rate, the second friend builds a raft to ferry more people to safety. *This can be equated to national initiatives such as TTO, infection and DVT prevention.* Where's the third friend? *That person is looking upstream, to prevent people from falling into the river in the first place* [9].

THINKING ABOUT THE WAY WE DO HEALTHCARE

Upstream is where more healthcare providers need to go, says Manchanda. "The upstreamist's job is not to be the hero nurse, the hero doctor, the hero community health worker," he says. "Instead, it is to think about how to systematically understand and address the social determinants of health." To which I would add, improving the systemic shortcomings that impair healthcare engagement and efficiency. We are so occupied with delivering healthcare that we don't spend enough time thinking about how to improve the delivery of that healthcare. The World Health Organisation identifies thinking about the underlying characteristics and relationships of health systems as a powerful tool for guiding sound, synergistic investments to target healthcare's weaknesses [10].

Fortunately, the aims of both clinicians and administrators are naturally aligned when it comes to both individual and systemic improvements. We want healthier, happier patients and healthcare workers. However, we need to be looking upstream to prevent healthcare problems occurring, to be at Hudson's Stage Five Generative Reliability, where 'safety is our way of doing business'. No one argues with doing what is right for patients, as demonstrated by ICHOM. The art of leadership is finding ways to make it easier for the healthcare team, clinical *and* non-clinical, to achieve their interrelated outcomes of reducing risk, reducing cost, and improving the healthcare experience [11].

Main Points:

1. Errors and waste are systematised in healthcare
2. Other industries have evolved with a higher priority on safety
3. Healthcare is too busy doing, with insufficient thinking about the way we 'do'
4. Barriers to change are cultural and systematic, and result in burnout
5. Clinician and administrator aims are more aligned than they first appear

7 WHY USE PURPOSE TO IMPROVE HEALTHCARE?

'If we want things to stay as they are, things will have to change.'

Giuseppe Tomasi

The great challenge in improving the safety and quality of healthcare is not in recognising problems, opportunities or possible solutions. It is in the implementation — in changing the ways that healthcare systems operate, so that the workplace is improved for clinical staff, and patients experience better care. Making these changes at a grassroots level has measurably great results. In essence, local improvements lead to improved engagement and efficiency, and reduced risk and cost in healthcare delivery [1, 2].

COORDINATION OF IMPROVEMENT MEASURES

Traditional improvement initiatives focus on isolated measures that ignore local context. As discussed in the previous chapter, 'context' is a smorgasbord of local, regional and national factors that, unless aligned, result in indigestion for implementers. Approaching a change or improvement programme as an opportunity to improve the healthcare experience for staff and patients improves alignment and success significantly [1, 2].

As clinical experts, doctors and nurses have a responsibility to optimise both the clinical and non-clinical parts of healthcare.

Optimising the non-clinical parts of healthcare is not part of clinical training. However, they are interdependent - one supports and affects the other. Clinicians can't devolve the non-clinical aspects of healthcare completely to administrators. As highlighted, professional management in healthcare is only decades old - unlike healthcare, which has been evolving for over one thousand years [3].

Furthermore, administrators can't ignore their effects on clinical workflows. Non-clinical aspects of healthcare delivery, such as the physical work environment, supply chains, and user experience for healthcare workers and patients, affect the clinical aspects of healthcare delivery enormously. Accordingly, improving the healthcare experience improves patient/customer satisfaction, as well as the work satisfaction, efficiency and effectiveness of healthcare workers - in the same way that improving worker/user experience has been found to have multiplicative benefits in other industries [1, 2, 4, 5].

WHAT'S SO HARD?

Unfortunately, in healthcare, we see administrative requirements most often in a negative way. Externally imposed requirements are often delivered by edict, rather than by engaging those tasked with implementation. Healthcare has many moving parts. Its processes tend not to move in an orderly fashion, and require many staff in disparate locations. See Figure 9 for considerations around operations. Typically, this is used as an excuse for a different standard of user experience in healthcare - we compare against our own, instead of what's possible externally and internationally. This is true for both patient and worker. It is ironic that an industry purported to be about caring too often delivers a sterile clinical experience instead.

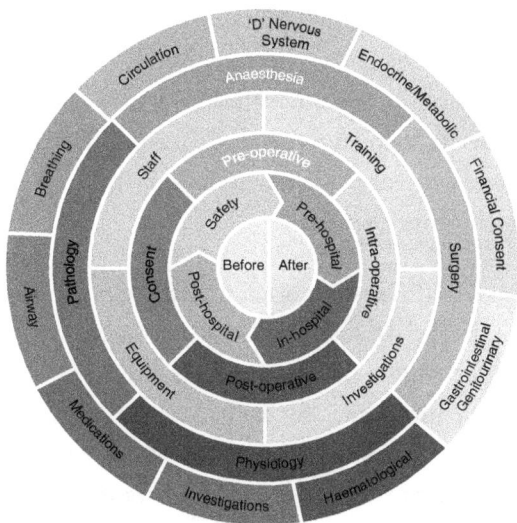

FIGURE 9   Perioperative Considerations

A systematic review of the use of patient experience data to improve quality in healthcare was equivocal in its findings, despite authors of individual papers reporting improvements and the success of ICHOM [6,7]. Interestingly, both Ritz-Carlton and Disney have measured and run courses on improving the patient experience in healthcare as a means to reduce risk and cost, not just to improve satisfaction scores [8].

WHO KNOWS BEST?

This raises the question – should healthcare benchmark healthcare services? If we really want the best for our patients, shouldn't we find best practice whatever the industry, and evaluate its utility for healthcare? Fortunately, making a connection between healthcare and hospitality is not a huge shift. Both hospitals and hotels admit (check-in) and discharge (check out) patients (customers). However, we do need to be mindful that a hospital admission differs from an hotel in that it is usually 'involuntary hospitality', and that healthcare is a calling, as opposed to a service job [9]. A patient is not just another customer.

In this sense, healthcare is more akin to the standout companies in service sectors – such as Ritz-Carlton and Disney [3, 8]. Similarly, the choices of patients regarding clinicians and healthcare facilities can be likened to customers choosing luxury goods – their perceptions of value are paramount. In both cases, purpose is more important than function. Fantastic food does not make up for disregarding the patient call bell. Modern décor does little to lessen the pain of lack of information. Patients have a simple need - caring and knowledgeable staff. This is true regardless of the patient's gender, age or cultural background. [10]

A NEW WAY OF THINKING

How do we coordinate so many moving parts to deliver a consistent caring clinical experience? Systems-thinking helps us to see the glue that binds the parts. For enterprises generally, and healthcare in particular, putting Purpose before Function is the missing element. Too often we forget that healthcare is a higher calling, and that this is what drives us. Healthcare systems usually place and measure technical excellence (function) ahead of purpose (e.g. a great healthcare experience). A slow burnout results for clinicians, who feel driven harder and harder for reasons that steadily recede into distant memory. Dissatisfaction results for patients, with adequate clinical outcomes instead of *outstanding*.

Purpose is what differentiates the insular 'we're as good as the next hospital' approach from the 'we aim to be the best' approach. It reflects strategy, rather than execution. Here are some further considerations that help us to ensure our purpose is reflected in what we do [7, 9-12]:

1. **First and Last Impressions Count.** These are readily fixed in the memory, and affect perception of related and subsequent events. Adverse events are diminished in the setting of good service, and amplified by poor patient service experiences.

2. **Patient-Centred Care.** This means finding ways to shift the convenience of healthcare delivery to the patient, rather than the traditional approach of convenience to the healthcare facility and worker. Telemedicine is one option; the patient does not have to travel to the healthcare provider, or wait for their arrival, and the healthcare provider is able to choose the time and place of meeting [13]. Chapters 9 and 10 expand on these concepts.

3. **Little Things Matter.** Raised eyebrows, poor dress standards and lack of eye contact send a powerful, albeit unintentional, message to patients; namely, that they are less important. This is true when on-site, or in uniform, whether on- or off-duty.

4. **The Value of (near) Real-Time Feedback.** The ubiquity of technology and devices means patients and their loved

ones can comment on their experiences in real-time. Naturally, it is best if a facility provides its own mechanism, in preference to unmoderated social and other media. The ability to obtain feedback that is acted upon is the quickest, cheapest, most consistent way to create a good impression. The facility will quickly learn the extent to which purpose, function, being patient-centred, and discovering the little things that matter to patients are being pursued.

To illustrate the last point, a London hospital was concerned that its patients were risking dehydration, despite provision of water at the bedside. Consumption appeared appropriate, so to understand what other factors may be at play, a survey was conducted. It transpired that the colour of the drinking glasses made it difficult to perceive depth. As a result, they were being knocked over frequently. Refills made water consumption appear adequate, when in fact the carpet was consuming a good proportion of the water.

HOW DO WE CONTROL LOCAL VARIATION?

Healthcare, and many other industries, have perpetuated the myth that creativity, or creative solutions to problems, and structure are incompatible [14]. Creativity has become synonymous with uncontrollable geniuses, and ultimate ruin. The reality is that rigid structure also ensures eventual ruin, as has occurred for many newspapers, and is occurring for traditional healthcare provision today. Balancing creativity and structure is critical in any workplace to optimise engagement, efficiency and empowerment of staff.

Using accepted and proven methodologies for capturing and evaluating creativity provides the structure necessary for a balance between the two. It also ensures team member buy-in and increased employee engagement, essential ingredients for reducing healthcare risk and cost [15]. One caveat is to ensure that decision makers have early involvement with the development process, to maximise the chances of developing successful projects.

Examples of methodologies that balance creativity and structure include Agile and Lean. These are explored in depth by a US/ Japanese collaboration, The Conference for Healthcare, now into its sixth year [16]. An outstanding success story comes from the Virginia Mason Medical Centre (VMMC), which has simultaneously reduced risk and cost, and improved the user experience for patients and staff. The centre was in the bottom quartile of healthcare institutions, and is now in the top 1% of US hospitals [2, 17]. Chapter 14 provides guidance on finding purpose for a healthcare enterprise.

The top three problems cited as 'solved' at VMMC were surgical setup improvements, venous thromboembolism prophylaxis regimen adherence, and avoiding medication errors. Importantly, these advances were achieved through including front-line administrative personnel, to tackle the non-clinical aspects of ensuring these clinical outcomes. A sense of shared purpose led to improved engagement, empowerment and efficiency, with the resultant benefits multiplying beyond the 'problems solved'.

Main Points:

1. Healthcare is good at recognising short-comings
2. Healthcare is poor at implementing improvements
3. Healthcare is insular
4. Systems thinking coordinates clinical and non-clinical requirements
5. Local input improves project outcomes

Section II

WHAT

8 CLINICIAN ENGAGEMENT

'The most dangerous kind of waste is the waste we do not recognize.'

Shigeo Shingo

For healthcare improvement to work we have to engage clinicians. To use a term from Deming, widely acknowledged as the leading management thinker in the field of quality, clinicians are healthcare's so-called 'smart cogs'. They are frontline workers who not just understand - they *own* the processes of care. Despite (or because of) this, it is difficult to get clinicians to see a new future. Fear, uncertainty and doubt about change make clinicians 'historically encumbered' resulting in a 'demoralised workforce' that is resistant to change. Fortunately, recognising this as a problem points us towards a solution [1].

What does 'engagement' mean with respect to clinicians? It can be conceptualised as an ongoing, two-way social process in which both the individual *and* organisational/cultural components are considered. This acknowledges the clinician as a 'smart cog' in the machine that is healthcare delivery. It also respects the needs of the organisation. Ongoing learning, one from the other, maximises the potential for both [2].

INTERDEPENDENCE

One way to engage clinicians, both allied and medical, is to get them to see the healthcare delivery *system* as a clinical tool that can alter healthcare outcomes, alongside their more familiar therapies. As such, it is an additional tool for improving clinical outcomes, not just an abstract construct of healthcare managers. As quality improvement is the science of process management – a tenet of Deming – it behoves us to explain this to clinicians, and to include *process* quality improvement measures alongside *clinical* quality improvement measures [1].

As part of explaining the importance of systems and processes, it is critical to ensure that clinicians and administrators understand that 'managing care' means managing the *process* of care, not managing the people contributing to the processes. In this way, clinicians can start to see how their contributions to process improvement help *them*, as well as clinical care and patients [1].

HOW DO WE ENGAGE CLINICIANS?

Clinicians are typically individualistic, of above average intelligence, highly educated and extraordinarily committed. Visiting Medical Officers (VMO's or 'Visiting Doctors') are a variant species to Employed Doctors. Both may coexist at public (governmental) and private medical facilities. Different expectations result from the formal employment contract versus informal visiting arrangements. A clinician may be employed at a public/governmental facility, and visit a private/non-government facility - and exhibit different behaviours at each.

Nonetheless, engaging clinicians in improving the healthcare delivery system is most effectively achieved by providing tools and systems to unlock their leadership capabilities. Key elements in developing highly effective clinician leadership include [2-4]:

1. **A well articulated vision and philosophy.** This should include the facility's purpose in their area of healthcare delivery, its identity and its positioning in the market (Chapter 14). This is an important shift in thinking, from reactive problem-solving to proactive future-building. It helps to articulate the gap between the present reality and the desired future state, to inspire innovation and collaboration for potentially challenging, long-term goals [5].

2. **A formalised selection process:** openness and transparency are important to build trust and to foster collaboration. These are pre-conditions for motivating clinicians (and other staff) to commit to long-term goals that drive innovation and improvement throughout the organisation.

3. **Measurable criteria:** clinicians are interested in real patients and real challenges, rather than theoretical. Hence basing improvement projects on actual and/or near-miss adverse events is more effective, particularly if the events were reported by clinician peers. Administrators are familiar with Deming's statement, 'If you cannot measure it, you cannot improve it' which aligns well with clinicians' use of clinical studies to improve healthcare interventions.

4. **Applied knowledge:** Clinicians prefer specific applications and projects rather than theory. Thus the IHI's pragmatic PDSA (Plan-Do-Study-Act) improvement cycle adapted from Deming is highly effective as it utilises incremental, iterative improvements where the benefit is clear (Figure 10 and Chapter 15) [1, 6].

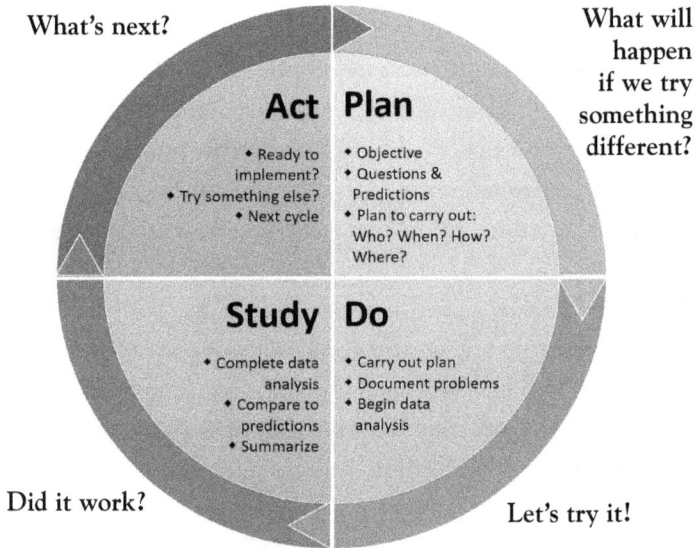

What's next?

What will happen if we try something different?

Act
- Ready to implement?
- Try something else?
- Next cycle

Plan
- Objective
- Questions & Predictions
- Plan to carry out: Who? When? How? Where?

Study
- Complete data analysis
- Compare to predictions
- Summarize

Do
- Carry out plan
- Document problems
- Begin data analysis

Did it work?

Let's try it!

FIGURE 10   PDSA Cycle for Learning and Improvement

5. **Self-awareness development** - emotional intelligence: Effective leaders are able to see themselves as others see them. This assists discovery and resolution of conflict. Self-awareness is an area of weakness in healthcare training, with a consequence of suppressed ingrained

conflict. However, clinicians like measurable competencies that relate to leadership, in order to build on strengths and improve weaknesses. Utilising strengths correlates with personal and professional fulfilment, promotes dialogue and assists in uncovering and resolving conflict [7, 8].

6. **Discernment between leadership and management.** In its simplest definition, leadership focuses more on thinking - longer term strategy, trends and obstacles, whereas management is more about short-term doing - effective, stable and predictable implementation. Differentiating between the two, and dedicating time to leadership, assists clinicians to 'work on' improving healthcare delivery processes at the facility, rather than only 'working in' the otherwise unchanging delivery of that healthcare. As above, this promotes dialogue and assists in uncovering and resolving conflict. Innovative outcomes often occur with the resulting collaboration yielding a sum greater than the parts [9].

7. **Learning and teaching.** The highest performing organisations and people are ones that are continuously learning and teaching throughout the organisation. This raises the intellectual and emotional intelligence of the organisation in a self-reinforcing cycle. Frequent and face-to-face contact is required to establish rapport, mutual trust, openness and collaboration. However, this is frequently missing in healthcare institutions. Contact allows clinicians to develop and apply leadership skills collectively, with each other and with the facility. Altruistic behaviour is promoted, assisting development of collective leadership [4, 5].

8. **Understanding of clinician work– life balance.** There
    is often little distinction for a clinician between personal
    and professional life, as they are so intertwined. A clinician
    is unable to discard a patient at 5:30 pm, as it is not in the
    patient's best interest to do so. Similarly, the demands of
    treating patients mean that maintaining a regular schedule
    is problematic. Consequently, scheduling meetings around
    the clinician and delivering flexible learning materials
    are most effective. Ways to achieve this include webinars
    that can be viewed wherever the clinician happens to find
    themselves, and podcasts that can be listened to while doing
    other activities, such as exercising.

WORKING INDEPENDENTLY

The *modus operandi* by administration least likely to generate a
constructive response is to use a command and control approach,
or the 'big stick'. This approach arises when a healthcare
organisation's functions are considered in isolation, rather than
as part of a complex, adaptive system. Changes in isolation may
well be ignored by clinicians, due to unwanted consequences
or unclear objectives. Clinician autonomy is reinforced by the
perception that the primary determinant of clinical outcomes
is the healthcare provider, in both the patient's mind and the
healthcare provider's. The complexity of the healthcare setting,
and factors such as processes, other staff and infrastructure all
affect outcomes [9].

Healthcare leaders may then be challenged by clinicians who
make statements such as, 'I just don't think XX is that important'.
Understanding the interactions between different parts of

the healthcare system assists both clinician and administrator in uncovering new and valuable capabilities. Purpose and capabilities in healthcare delivery, rather than the minutiae of service delivery, thus becomes important in aligning the interests of staff and doctors with patients and the healthcare facility [10].

It is also not helpful to 'name and shame', as this belittles the role of the doctor. A passive-aggressive response ensues and the clinician-administration relationship deteriorates further. Clinician burnout, or worse, is the longer-term outcome of this scenario, and is a leading indicator of poor healthcare system performance [7-11, 13].

PURPOSE OVER FUNCTION

How can we use 'Purpose' to assist in a difficult encounter with a healthcare provider who professes that they 'don't give a damn' about compliance requirements or hospital targets? An often-quoted example, supported by statistics, is hand-washing to reduce the incidence of hospital-acquired (transferred) infection. Doctors consistently score lower than other healthcare workers, and according to Australia's most recent safety and quality report have improved less as well, despite coming off a low base. Now, doctors understand in detail about transmission of infection, the tragedy of Semmelweis notwithstanding. Why then do they consistently score lower on what is a simple task [14, 15]?

We know from implementation theory and practice that any process that adds complexity has a lower success rate. This should not be surprising given the complex and adaptive nature of healthcare delivery. Unfortunately, hand-washing suffers from this 'shortcoming'– hand-washing adds a task before *and* after interaction with the patient. This can be a major barrier to adoption of consistent hand-washing. Intellectual understanding of the importance is therefore insufficient – emotional engagement is required [9].

This can be achieved by:

- **Involving the clinician(s)** in formulating the solution, through PDSA cycles or other institution-specific models;
- **Patient satisfaction.** Doctors are more likely to comply if they are aware that their patients disapprove of skipping hand-washing (Chapter 10); and
- **Peer comparisons.** Clinicians are competitive by nature. Making the lowest outliers aware privately that they are below their peer average assists self-regulation. High outliers can be asked to formulate recommended solutions for their peers (Chapter 12).

Active clinician involvement is essential to the success of healthcare improvement programs, whether the focus is on non-clinical aspects of healthcare delivery or on clinical improvement. This not only translates the initiative into language that clinicians can identify with, it also helps uncover improvements not previously considered. In this way we improve engagement and efficiency, and reduce risk and cost in a way that creates a better work experience for the clinician. A virtuous cycle results [16].

Main Points:

1. Clinicians own care processes
2. Understanding the effect of non-clinical processes on clinical outcomes teaches their importance
3. Managing care manages processes - not people
4. Understanding the interdependence of clinical processes and administrative processes helps improve outcomes
5. Learning leadership skills helps clinicians, and the organisation, achieve their objectives

9 VIRTUAL CARE DELIVERY MODELS

> 'When solving problems, dig at the roots instead of just hacking at the leaves.'
>
> Anthony J. D'Angelo

'Virtual care' delivery models are a mainstream phenomenon redefining accessibility, availability and affordability of healthcare for patients worldwide. Virtual care is care that is delivered outside the traditional face-to-face healthcare model. It offers benefits to healthcare providers, patients and the healthcare system. First and foremost, personalised healthcare can be delivered cost-effectively where and when the patient requires it. Second, care provider expertise can be available even when the provider isn't. Third, collaboration is facilitated to improve information sharing, workflows and outcomes – both clinical and financial. Engagement, efficiency and empowerment are the results [1].

THE TECH TRANSFORMATION

Digital networks and technology make the transformation from reactive disease treatment to proactive health optimisation possible. They permit predictive, preventative, personalised and participatory care - so-called 'P4Medicine'. Virtual care is an important component of this, and encompasses telemedicine, enhanced or augmented reality, virtual reality and artificial intelligence [2].

Virtual healthcare (Figure 11) is delivered remotely by a clinician, using voice via telephony, or video and voice via computer network on smartphone, tablet or computer. Patient-end devices can be used to provide additional information to the clinician. While these may be specialised devices such as ECG's or pulse oximeters, or smart-watches, they provide raw data -without analysis. This is telemedicine, and it is increasingly utilised by clinicians and patients to heighten convenience and quality of care [3].

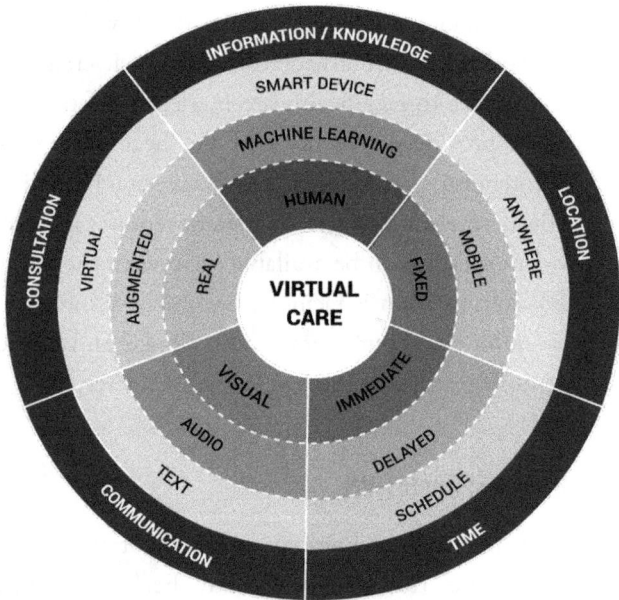

FIGURE 11   Redesign Inputs

In a similar vein, remote monitoring can alert carers when a person with chronic care needs may require help. Sensors and simple predictive analytics can be used to generate alerts when movement is not detected or remains confined to one room. In 2016 Australia's CSIRO showed cost savings of 24-46% in a twelve month pilot of home monitoring, and reduced mortality of 40%. Savings arose from better coordination of care, and reduced unnecessary healthcare costs, hospitalisations and length of stay. User acceptance was over 80% for both patients and clinicians, including the elderly. We should be using virtual healthcare more [4].

HEAD-UP DISPLAYS FOR HEALTHCARE

Superimposing digital information via smart glasses onto a viewer's vision of the physical world enhances their reality, in much the same way as the 'head-up display' in a car allows the driver to see their speed without taking their eyes off the road. An extension of this is to use a physical nurse and a projected doctor to make home visits. This 'mixed reality' service was developed by Silverchain in partnership with Microsoft and launched in Western Australia in 2017 [5,6]. Specialised devices such as ECG's or pulse oximeters, or applications on the patient's smart-watch, smartphone, tablet or computer can record physiologic data and report remotely. Advanced healthcare is projected into the home more efficiently and at lower cost than with traditional doctor home visits.

Alternatively, patients or carers can research information electronically that is matched with varying fidelity to their age, gender, race and any diseases. Virtual reality imagery can be used to explain concepts or demonstrate symptoms. Care can then be escalated to video consultations, referral for physical consultations, or ambulance transfer to a medical centre if indicated. 'Virtual' providers are used both by individuals, and by company healthcare systems for employees. Billions of consultations have been delivered in this manner, very cheaply and at a time and place convenient to the patient [7, 8].

PREDICTIVE HEALTHCARE

At the digital extreme, remote care is being augmented by applications on a patient's smart-watch or smartphone. These applications use machine learning to analyse physiologic data such as heart rate and breathing rate, comparing it to activity levels to predict physical disease. These applications can prompt patients to contact care up to a week before they become aware of a pending problem. The protocols have been validated for heart attacks, sleep apnoea, airways disease and irregular heart rhythms that can cause stroke. While these applications are a huge step forward, they are not yet perfect. For example, it is interesting to note that the emotional distress of seeing your favourite sporting team lose a grand final can simulate an impending heart attack [9, 10].

The business case for virtual care for the healthcare system is clear from the CSIRO data, among others. For individual healthcare enterprises, the business case includes expanding the reach of both physical facilities and clinicians to optimise revenue possibilities, and reduce cost of delivery, especially in the face of geographic spread. In Australia, it is ideal for improving services to remote and rural communities, and individuals [1, 4].

The limitations to uptake of virtual care models are human rather than technological. The CSIRO project reported on the effect of workplace culture, and of capacity for innovation and organisational change management. In integrating a new model of telehealth care with long established service models they clearly demonstrated that success related more to on-site clinical leadership, capacity to accommodate change and the flexibility of existing processes and systems. There was little impact from technical issues associated with the telehealth monitoring equipment, or patient compliance to monitoring schedules. [4, 11]

Consequently, an approach to improving uptake is required. The recommended model is to focus improvements around the patient, as this reduces barriers for clinical and non-clinical staff alike. Leadership training for clinical staff further improves the likelihood of success for a team-based, collaborative approach.

Main Points:

1. Virtual care delivery models are a mainstream phenomenon worldwide, delivered without traditional geographic or time supply constraints.
2. Significant improvements in outcomes and cost occur with the addition of virtual healthcare
3. Extra information via head-up displays improves the carer and patient interaction
4. Barriers to uptake are human rather than technological
5. Predictive learning on your watch or smart-phone can save your life

10 PATIENT-CENTRED CARE

> 'The first rule of any technology used in a business is that automation applied to an efficient operation will magnify the efficiency. The second is that automation applied to an inefficient operation will magnify the inefficiency.'
>
> **Bill Gates**

Patient-centred care has become a buzzword. It was promoted in 1988 by the Picker Institute to shift healthcare's focus away from disease and onto patients and their families. Unfortunately, like 'staff engagement' it receives lip-service and superficial interventions, such as improved interior decoration or glossy brochures. The processes are still hospital-centric, they just look better. This is a bit like putting lipstick on a pig [1].

IS THIS ANOTHER FAD?

Patient-centred care is important – it's not just customer service, and it's not just a passing fad. The International Consortium for Health Outcomes Measurement was established recently to help transform health care systems by measuring and reporting patient outcomes in a standardised way (www.ichom.org). So what does patient-centric really look like? When patients and their caregivers are full, active participants in their health decisions, the experience of care, and economic outcomes, can be substantially improved [1-4].

Patients want information and compassion. Compassion means respect and dignity, and individualisation of the patient experience. Not so long ago, caring and compassion were the only treatments available for many illnesses. In a rapid turnover facility with many similar procedures, this can be forgotten unintentionally. It might be the thousandth time for the clinician or the nurse, however, it is usually the first time for the patient [2, 3].

SAFETY AND SATISFACTION

Communication is a key aspect of healthcare, not just for patient experience. It is a key safety mechanism during transitions of care. Given that the patient is the only person always present, their involvement is logical as well as compassionate. This becomes magnified in chronic conditions, where poor discharge planning and inadequate community support results in earlier, more frequent, preventable readmissions [2, 5-7].

Healthcare frequently offers multiple interventions for a given condition, each with its own benefits, side effects, and costs. Identifying the most valuable intervention for a given patient requires communication with, and participation by, the patient. Patients need to be well informed about their options, and clinicians need to be aware of each patient's context - their individual circumstances, preferences, and needs. Patient perceptions of personalisation correlate with adherence to treatment regimes. Conversely, healthcare skills are compromised when a patient perceives that the carer does not care [3].

QUALITY CARE MEANS CARING

Traditionally, healthcare has concentrated on hard metrics, such as risk of infections or leg clots, to measure quality of care. It has been assumed that demonstrating a high quality of care results in patient loyalty. However, this is not completely the case. Up to half of patients report inadequate information about advantages and disadvantages of treatment options, with a feeling of inadequate control over their choices. Quality of human *experience* correlates best with loyalty – as is the case with other industries [8-10].

These factors contributed to the establishment of ICHOM. When seeking treatment, patients want to know what their life will be like after treatment. This is not just about symptoms – it is the ability to take care of oneself, to work, and to lead a fulfilling life.

WHAT MATTERS TO PATIENTS

On the downside, a negative personal experience with a healthcare provider (or healthcare facility) alters perception of events before and after the episode of care. Problems become magnified and any good experiences are diminished. It is well recognised that one bad event requires seven good events to 'balance it out'. A poor patient experience may result in a patient seeking care elsewhere, and an increased likelihood of litigation. Approximately 7% of patients have switched healthcare providers due to poor customer experience, according to Accenture research. This switching can translate to a loss of more than US$100 million in annual revenue per large hospital [3,9].

The role of technology for patient engagement has grown. However, it is an under-utilised avenue in healthcare. Raised patient expectations come from a new standard of customer service in industries such as banking. Privacy is often cited as a barrier to electronic communications in healthcare, although there are similar considerations and requirements in financial services [8, 9].

REQUESTING FEEDBACK DEMONSTRATES CARING

Patient satisfaction and patient-reported experience measures are also an important feedback mechanism for clinicians. This can be provided in a de-identified manner for clinicians to assist in building their practice, their leadership and their relationship with the healthcare facility. The natural competitiveness of clinicians means low-rating clinicians, when provided with a confidential comparison against their peers, will seek out ways to improve their rating.

When patients perceive that their healthcare provider cares, they are more likely to be giving of signs and symptoms, and receptive of treatment directions. The act of seeking out patient-reported experience measures demonstrates caring. A simple example is to ask, 'what matters to you?' rather than, 'what is the matter?' According to the IHI, in many cases this has improved the individual's care plan, enhanced the patient's relationship with their healthcare provider and improved healthcare outcomes. Patients and customers are less concerned with treatment problems per se – they are more concerned with how they are looked after, should any problems arise [1, 10, 11].

COMMUNICATION MEANS TWO-WAY

A recent white paper developed jointly by a physician organisation, the American Association for Physician Leadership, and a patient organisation, The Beryl Institute, found that both physicians and patients want communication to improve. Patients often understand less than their clinicians believe they understand, and as highlighted above this leads to problems with their care. Patients also want more time to discuss diagnoses and treatment options [15]. Important factors in patient-centred care are summarised in Figure 12.

FIGURE 12   Patient-Centred Care

Interestingly, improving the patient experience affects clinicians in positive and important ways. The same paper recognises the mutual need for, and importance of, collaboration and honest dialogue [15]:

1. **Power and influence increase.** Doctors who are regarded as exceptional or pre-eminent in their ability to relate to patients have more power and influence. Staff and healthcare providers value their opinion more highly than those healthcare providers who do not have empathy.

2. **Risk of burnout decreases.** Rather than just applying their intellectual skills, the healthcare provider is utilising their human skills. Consequently, they better perceive the impact they have on those around them, not just patients. Professional and personal satisfaction increases, and a positive feedback loop is created.

While subjective, social media is still highly valued by patients and consumers as a source of information: either provided by people they know and trust; or that they believe can be taken at face value; or which they can use to research further. Healthcare facilities and clinicians are advised to monitor social media and have a procedure to acknowledge and respond to feedback, both positive and negative. Again, patients are less concerned with negative reviews than with the healthcare provider's response to those reviews.

Patient-reported experience measures can be used to customise quality improvement initiatives, such as changing patient educational materials or admission processes, in ways that matter to patients. While the feedback is often subjective in nature, it also serves to educate and inform staff about the importance of the patient experience when improving quality and efficiency in healthcare. Tackling waiting times is an example of an organisation-wide quality improvement measure that demonstrates care for the patient as a person, whilst also saving the organisation money. These can include waiting times for appointments, or for transitions from one care area to another [3, 16].

Patient-centred care at an organisational level means transparency. Public reporting is now a reality, through Government and Health fund reporting of public and private hospitals and healthcare providers. Poor reports are a powerful reason to change. Good reports are powerful for marketing.

Shared decision-making, then, is the pinnacle of patient-centred care. This is the whole of the patient's experience, not just satisfaction scores, and not 'merely' good clinical outcomes. Training staff in the 'patient experience' improves efficiency and reduces mistakes. When we look at other industries, the most successful and enduring companies are ones that listen to what the consumer wants and needs, rather than telling them what they should want or need [4, 10, 12-14].

Main Points:

1. Patient-centred means care, compassion, quality and cost-effectiveness

2. Technical excellence is not a surrogate for caring excellence

3. What matters to patients differs from healthcare workers

4. Requesting feedback demonstrates caring - to patients, staff and clinicians

5. Communication is a two-way process, for patients, staff and clinicians

11 WHY DO IMPROVEMENTS FAIL?

> 'The science of medicine is thousands of years old. The discipline of management sciences, which includes the study of leadership, is less than 100 years old. Management sciences applied to healthcare is still in its infancy.' [1]

It is little wonder that the healthcare system is dysfunctional. It started as a scarce resource - and still is in the developing world. It was rewarded for effort, and paid for the volume of patients seen or operations performed - and it continues to be. It has grown into a behemoth consuming 10-15% of GDP in most countries today. Attempts to rationalise healthcare have fallen foul of deep-rooted (and deep-pocketed) vested interests, and Fear, Uncertainty and Doubt relating to change (the FUD Principle) [2].

The purpose of healthcare, to optimise the health (and therefore productivity) of the population, has been forgotten by many of its participants. Large chunks of healthcare have become corporatised and the purpose slowly changed to maximising short-term profit for shareholders. However, prioritising people and maximising profit aren't incompatible, as shown by earlier examples of successful businesses that put customers and employees first in order to maximise shareholder value over the long-term.

ISOLATED VS INTERDEPENDENT IMPROVEMENTS

Healthcare has been looking for ways to improve quality and operational efficiency while cutting costs for three decades. Improvements that are logical at head office level often do not fix a problem at the individual level. As discussed in Chapter 4, changes that increase profit do not necessarily decrease the healthcare spend due to perverse incentives and the 'wrong pockets' problem [3].

Hospitals are complex, adaptive systems. They have evolved over time, with unique influences and events that have shaped their personalities or culture. Further, they are dynamic systems that adapt to accommodate the fluidity of constantly changing daily work. Consequently, when organisational improvements complicate the daily tasks of an individual, an otherwise logical and appropriate improvement is likely to fail.

As revealed in the opening quote, the cavalry sent to fix healthcare, administrators, are still learning the healthcare ropes. Rather than containing costs, an increasingly weighty administrative burden has paralleled rising healthcare costs (Chapter 4). Individual healthcare function, unit or enterprise optimisations haven't translated to healthcare system optimisation. Increased administrative leadership hasn't resulted in a societal benefit, despite this being a community expectation [4, 5].

BALANCE GLOBAL INITIATIVES WITH LOCAL NEEDS

Delivering improvements in healthcare requires the alteration of processes within complex social systems that change over time in both predictable and unpredictable ways. Research findings highlight the influential effect that local context can have on the success of an intervention [5, 6]. Practical experience also tells us this, whether it be introducing the Surgical Safety Checklist or discussing a change in practice with peers in the light of new experience [6-8]. This is the rationale for the use of PDSA Cycles for iterative learning and improvement.

While context is fundamental to understanding and addressing the safety and quality issues facing healthcare in Australia and elsewhere, it is often poorly defined as 'the setting in which care takes place'.

Specific organisational factors include [9-11]:

- Leadership from top management,
- Organisational culture,
- Data infrastructure and information systems, and
- Years involved in quality improvement (QI) measures.

The above reviews also identified potentially important individual and team factors: physician involvement in QI, team motivation to change, resources for QI, and QI team leadership. These more established mechanisms include clinical guidelines, audit and peer review. Context is important when analysing and understanding culture, devising and implementing change, and ensuring care is patient-centred and culturally appropriate.

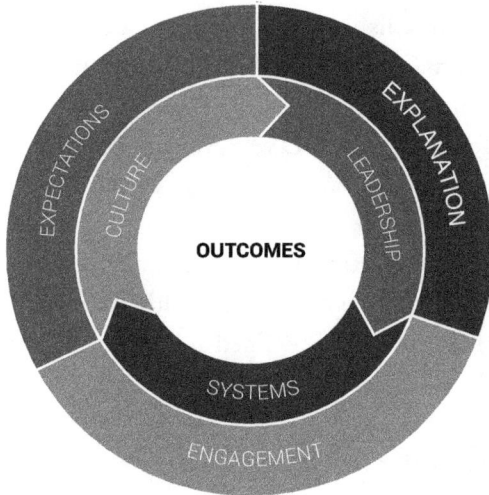

FIGURE 13   Prerequisites for Improvement

Without the organisational factors, motivation at the individual/team level withers and dies. Overarching both of these is the impact of high level health service interventions such as regulation, and public/private funding. Without alignment, these processes will impair each other. When used in a coordinated way, synergy is more likely [11].

WHO USES HEALTHCARE?

Healthcare involves everyone as consumers, carers and patients at one time or another. Many of us have dual roles as patients and healthcare workers (clinical or administrative). Thus the context, and by extension user experience, of both the patient and healthcare worker warrant consideration when devising healthcare improvement programmes.

This means that healthcare improvement measures and their implementation cannot be replicated simplistically. 'Magic bullet' interventions do not exist – they will not reliably deliver consistent improvements [12].

As a large and mature industry, healthcare naturally resists change. Fear, uncertainty and doubt are natural responses to large external forces that threaten to bring inevitable change. As noted by Chase, these were the very human responses in the media industry when faced with the external threat of digital media. The media industry had been essentially unchanged for 100 years, using physical printing presses to produce physical newspapers. Digital media overtook physical, and now digital media spending surpasses not only physical newspapers, but also broadcast television. Both of these predictions were laughed at [2].

As a larger and older industry, healthcare is even more of a challenge to change than media. For interventions to be effective, they need to be complex and multi-faceted, at the same time as being developed iteratively to adapt to the local context, and to respond to unforeseen obstacles and unintended effects [12-15].

THE HUMAN FACTOR

Knowing that fear, uncertainty and doubt are normal human responses to change prompts us to address them when implementing change programmes. A typical implementation plan labours under the misapprehension of "command and control". This is destined to fail, because prior to training, clinicians were selected for their capacity for independent thought and then highly trained to integrate disparate pieces of information to diagnose – that is, working independently to reach independent conclusions. Clinicians dislike and resist external attempts at control because they are used to working independently [9, 11, 16].

The personal relationships patients often have with their healthcare providers (people and facilities) is another powerful source of resistance to change. Deference or a shared delusion that 'it has to be this way – because it always has been' reinforces resistance to change. This personal dimension was much weaker in media and other industries, and helps explain the glacial pace of change in healthcare.

Due to the inherent lack of understanding of each other's universe, clinicians and administrators tend to favour their own drivers for healthcare improvement. Both approaches are entirely logical, however they disregard the synergy that occurs by combining efforts. Worse, conflicts can arise, resulting in diminished efficiencies with poor outcomes and increased costs. This impairs the working environment for both clinicians and healthcare employees.

So, taking all of this into account, how do we reduce the risk of failure in our next project? Attempts to integrate clinical and commercial drivers fail for similar reasons to any other unsuccessful project, with errors magnified by the causes above.

There are three main domains:

1. **Expectations:** Inadequate definition of the scope and vision;
2. **Explanation:** An inadequately defined model for the change; and
3. **Engagement:** Inadequate programme management for the change.

Specific techniques to increase the success rate in healthcare improvement projects will be considered in the next chapters. One area commonly neglected is **physician leadership training.** Physicians are not trained or well experienced in considering financial aspects to treatment, because this can result in a natural conflict between what is best for the patient versus what is best for the healthcare system. There is also a moral hazard when different treatments result in different revenues for a facility or a practitioner. Consequently, a natural distrust of commercial discussions arises in the absence of appropriate governance and leadership training.

While it sounds obvious, the best way to minimise project implementation problems is to involve the people affected. Often this occurs too late in the project cycle. Using an iterative development plan starting in the pre-implementation phase uncovers potential people and resourcing problems early – with and by the people best positioned to solve them. Expectations are more clearly set, with repeated opportunities for explanation, and with engagement as part of the process rather than a desperately pursued outcome. Better project results follow, with unexpected productivity benefits from team formation and collaboration, and spontaneous solutions to problems not previously articulated. Often the worst problems yield the biggest benefits.

MAIN POINTS:

1. Healthcare's interdependencies complicate improvement programmes
2. It is important to balance high-level initiatives with local needs
3. Resistance to change is pervasive - for patients, staff and clinicians
4. The human factor is critical - healthcare affects everyone
5. Continually re-evaluate expectations, provide detailed explanations, and maximise opportunities for engagement

12 VARIATIONS IN CARE

'Watch the little things; a small leak will sink a great ship.'
Benjamin Franklin

Establishing the best use of funding appears to be the primary issue for affordable, available and accessible healthcare. We need to obtain better value with the funding at hand, rather than mindlessly pursue cost reductions in an inefficient system. Developed countries typically have ample funding available, however it is not used optimally as evidenced by waste estimates of 20% or more. Better use of funding enables us to independently decide what is appropriate care for whom, rather than using capacity restraints as a proxy for controlling care [1-3].

Identifying and analysing variations in care is one tool to tackle this issue. Variations in care is a wide term, especially when clinical inputs drive 20% of care outcomes, and non-clinical inputs drive 80% (Figure 14) [4]. It is important to remember that we are managing variations in care, not variations in people. A useful way of defining variation is as waste in care. Waste is anything that does not add value. Examples include waste of consumables, unnecessary movement of staff, patients or products from one area to another (and often back again), waiting, excessive holding of stock, repetition of a task and mismatching of the care required to services provided.

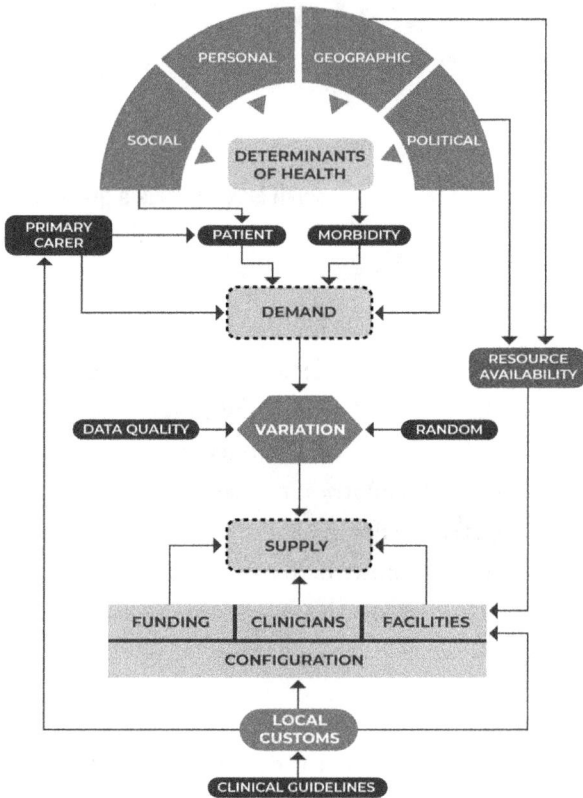

FIGURE 14   Variations in Care

A CASE STUDY

A colleague of mine constructed a radio-frequency identification (RFID) tracking system for hospital consumables. It monitors stock location and levels in real-time. The direct savings for a typical mid-size hospital in Victoria amounted to A\$1 million annually, through reduced stock levels and storage space. [10] Indirect savings multiply this figure, through less waiting for consumables, less waste and improved efficiency and engagement from staff. So there is a lot of room to improve clinical outcomes by targeting non-clinical inputs. This is where the importance of value improvement over cost reduction can be understood [5, 6].

PERVERSE INCENTIVES

The other big area for value improvement is in aligning incentives. Unfortunately, much of healthcare is funded by rewarding volume of services delivered. At best this creates a moral hazard to provide a service of equivocal benefit, because there is a financial incentive to do so. At worst, structures can be created solely to maximise the revenue obtainable from a healthcare population. This is applicable to suppliers, healthcare facilities, private payors and healthcare providers, simply because the system is so designed [7].

Unfortunately, 'variations in care' is usually applied in a narrow fashion, referring only to clinical care. Blaming people is only half of the story - systems are perfectly 'designed' to get the results they create. Clinicians are often concerned that when others manage variations in care, that it is a proxy tool for managing clinicians. In analysing variations in care, the questions typically asked are:

• Why is utilisation high in one area, and low in another area? and
• Is the care appropriate? [8]

A BROAD SCOPE

The variability of the complex adaptive system that is healthcare makes this analysis problematic. When clinical inputs drive 20% of care outcomes, and non-clinical inputs drive 80%, clinical-only analysis and recommendations are doomed to inadequacy. Further, the understanding of value provided to patients is incomplete. For example, expensive interventions are of no value to patients unless they add to their quality of life, and conversely, low clinical quality interventions can still be of value to a patient's quality of life [6].

A more powerful clinical analysis arises when including the system factors that determine healthcare outcomes. Commonly, analyses shy away from this apparently complex task, citing difficulty controlling variables ('context'). Or, analyses include many sites, with the result that the noise of many small variations cancels out the important few factors required for higher quality, lower cost care. This is akin to concluding a treatment doesn't 'work', when the error is patient or disease stage selection.

MAKING SENSE OF COMPLEXITY

How do we begin to understand the system factors at healthcare sites which deliver care that is cheaper and better than others? It is done by uncovering the sites that deliver higher quality care for lower unit cost – and then analysing those sites. From these learnings we start to see which interdependent variables are more influential at a particular site. Note that it is important when collecting data that analysis is not attempted at the point of care, as this leads to push-back from staff [5].

When a higher cost and/or lower quality site wishes to improve its metrics, an analysis is again required. Tabulating the results allows comparison with 'benchmark' sites, and variations can be identified. Variances should then be ranked according to ease or difficulty of modification. We can then target the more important, more easily modified variable(s). These are not necessarily the *most* important, as some variables may be difficult to modify. Securing improvements in other areas first builds the credibility and momentum to tackle more difficult areas. It may also be found that improvements in some areas ameliorate or lessen problems in other areas, due to the interdependency of healthcare systems.

WHAT OUTCOMES MATTER?

When addressing variations in care, it is important that the mindset is not merely about cost-reduction, but rather that it is about value creation or improvement. That is, avoid wide variations in care that do not improve outcomes, and/or do not matter to patients. These generate wasteful expenditure. We know that if we get patients healthier faster with better function, that outcomes are improved with lower costs [6].

Formulating and testing solutions is best done in an iterative fashion. Clinicians are used to iterative learning – it is how they acquired their medical knowledge and honed their clinical skills while training. However, after training they are often left adrift in a sea of doubt, with little feedback. This can be quite alienating, and can lead to hidden insecurity about performance. By fixing this problem with constructive, peer-designed and clinician-led feedback, such as the ICHOM Standard Sets, healthcare facilities can build their relationship with their clinician body. The work environment improves, patients benefit and risk, variation and cost in healthcare go down. Centres using the ICHOM system are found worldwide [6].

EXPECTATIONS, EXPLANATIONS AND ENGAGEMENT

Iterative improvement cycles permit organisational learning and fine-tuning of the improvement project – or early abandonment if the improvement project was inadequately constituted. It is a familiar construct to clinicians, who, as scientists, are trained to look narrowly at particular procedures, interventions or medications. The primary difference is that organisational improvement 'experiments' are shorter, self-contained and each informs the design of the next. When patient-reported outcomes are included, a culture of improvement follows, facilitating transparency and ongoing organisational improvement [6, 9].

The super-specialisation of healthcare means that speciality-matched clinicians must be involved in analysis to ensure understanding of treatment alternatives. Other disciplines, including administrative, help provide cognitive diversity to brain-storm novel solutions once a full understanding is achieved.

Simply by measuring and reporting variability in costs and outcomes, clinicians can become aware of the importance of improving value in healthcare delivery. By involving clinicians in analysing the two extremes, that is, high cost for no added benefit, and best outcomes for the least cost, both clinician and organisational learning can occur. As this collaborative process spreads the healthcare system improves. Variations in care outcomes decrease, cost and risk in care decrease, and the monetary and patient value of care delivered increases.

MAIN POINTS:

1. Manage variations in care, not variations in people. Non-clinical inputs drive up to 80% of variations, however are often overlooked

2. The system and its perverse incentives are part of the problem

3. Learning from the real world accommodates complexity, for benchmark sites, and for sites wishing to improve

4. Tackle expensive variations that do not improve outcomes, especially if they are not useful to patients

5. Iterative improvements accommodate expectations, improve explanation and engagement - and outcomes

---

HOW

13 COLLABORATIVE HEALTHCARE IMPROVEMENT

> 'It's the little things that make the big things possible. Only close attention to the fine details of any operation [systems] makes the operation first class.'
>
> **J. Willard Marriott Sr.**

The healthcare system is in a perfect storm of increasing demand, increasing complexity, technological advances, funding constraints, and dehumanisation, for both patients and healthcare workers. Demand for services outstrips the capacity of most countries' budgets. The population is ageing and medical problems are becoming more complex. However, a society's biggest problems are also its greatest opportunities.

WHY CHANGE NOW?

Healthcare delivery has reached a tipping point. Current models are unsustainable in the face of rising costs and reducing reimbursements. Healthcare is facing a transition via customer demand, facilitated by technology, from reactive treatment of disease to proactive optimisation of wellness. Patients are being assisted to coordinate (if not control) their own health management. How do we deal with the financial pressures, while positioning ourselves to manage patient input?

A common stumbling block to successfully improving healthcare is not in recognising problems, opportunities or possible solutions – it is in the failure to delve deeper and diagnose the cause, and in just dealing superficially with the symptoms. Not only this, but in bringing an improvement project to life insufficient attention is often given to understanding the intended and unintended consequences of proposed solutions. Systems thinking is an important and under-used tool for these issues [1].

Implementation involves changing the ways that health professionals behave and healthcare systems operate. Change introduces fear, uncertainty and doubt, resulting in resistance. As a result, most implementations fail to attain their objectives, especially in healthcare. How do we work with this natural response so that the workplace is improved, and patients experience better care?

HOW DO WE OVERCOME RESISTANCE?

Success is increased when the participants utilise their natural strengths and talents, on projects that hold meaning or purpose. Needs and roles ebb and flow with the demands of a project, forming and reforming social networks in an organic manner. This can blur the project's meaning or purpose. Defining and linking the facility's purpose with that of the project provides a defined framework to ensure the project and its tasks remain focused [2].

New models are required to ensure a collaborative, proactive approach to the delivery of healthcare. Development of a new model requires active collaboration among all involved:

- Patients
- Administrators
- Clinicians
- Family and friends
- Funders: government (state care, federal), private industry
- Regulators: government, medical board, professional colleges, de facto (health funds)
- Suppliers: equipment, prostheses, pharma

Each participant has multiple points of contact with the patient at different stages of their care. Many people are involved during these stages. For an optimum patient experience the touch points need to be coordinated around the service being provided, which is the care interaction. This means coordinating around the patient, not the convenience of the provider. However, ideally, the provider experience will feel centred around the provider as well. Inevitably, digital health is required to facilitate this individualised experience for all involved.

Previous chapters have discussed designing patient-centred care. Similarly, the other participants of the various healthcare interactions need to have a hand in optimising their own interactions. This means treating everyone, to some extent, like a customer of the enterprise.

WHAT IS THE COMMON FACTOR?

Digital healthcare is not the magic bullet. Prior to the introduction of digital tools, each user's experience needs to be optimised, with a process in place to permit continued optimisation during and after implementation of changes. Obtaining information from all the participants in any healthcare process is essential for design to add value. Engagement is created by feeding back information, so that it becomes a two-way process. This means that a 'learning and teaching' organisation can develop so that continual improvement becomes the way that business is done in the enterprise, continuing after a change project is completed [3].

With any large scale of change, a modular approach is best to determine what area provides most benefit to the enterprise - and is most feasible. Staged development can then occur, relating each stage to local conditions. This is of particular importance because the same symptoms can have different causes. Devolving implementation to local teams that utilise tools such as systems thinking enables improved diagnosis of the local underlying problems [1, 4]. Expectations, explanations and engagement become optimised, improving project success (Figure 15).

HOW DO WE COORDINATE TEAMS?

A coherent roadmap maintains stability during the change. How do we create the roadmap for change? As discussed above, this comes from a sense of purpose for the enterprise. Each project can then be tested against the 'purpose' to ensure relevance and congruity. Whatever the facility's purpose, our research shows that there are four essential components of a successful improvement programme. It must:

1. Improve healthcare outcomes,
2. Improve the healthcare experience for patients,
3. Improve the healthcare experience for healthcare providers, and
4. Improve budgets.

To achieve these outcomes, simplification of healthcare delivery is required. This means reducing and removing unnecessary and/ or duplicate workflows, and automating others to reduce and/ or remove the need for human intervention. This improves the healthcare experience for patients and healthcare providers alike, because effort is reduced. Consequently, engagement is improved and errors reduced. In turn, efficiency increases, along with budget outcomes. Improvement in facility reputation, sustained by ongoing improvement programmes, occurs. This attracts patient referrals and quality staff as a preferred healthcare provider and employer.

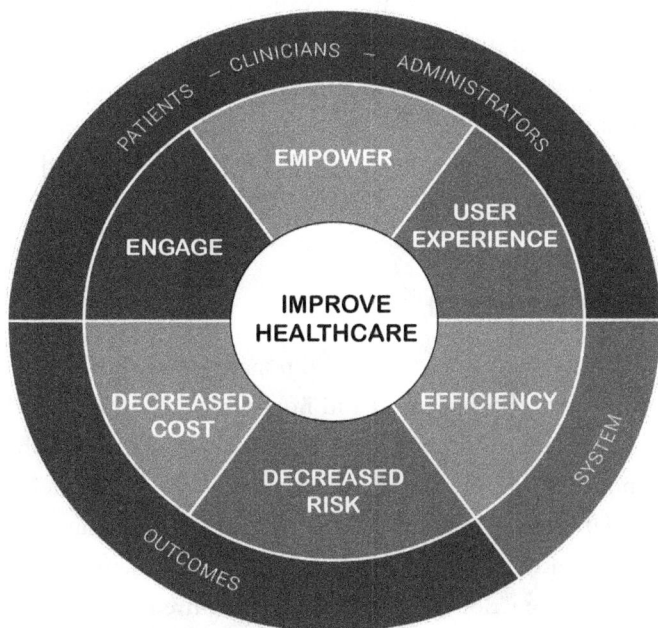

FIGURE 15   Collaboration

REDUCING COMPLEXITY

So, how do we reduce workflow complexity in order to pursue workflow process improvement? This requires innovation, and innovation needs collaboration by everyone involved in the process. Innovation used to be left to external experts and designers, however, they alone no longer have the detailed insights necessary for continued and/or more effective innovation.

Involving everyone in the innovation/improvement process has a bonus - collaboration increases engagement, a benefit to the organisation in its own right [2]. Words such as change, redesign, innovation and disruption can be confronting to the majority of healthcare workers, who desire continuity. Avoiding these terms and highlighting the collaborative nature of improving the workplace increases engagement, productivity and the likelihood of success.

LEADERSHIP REVISITED

Leadership is required at every step mentioned above. This is important for both clinical and non-clinical staff. New skills and behaviours are required. This training is well established for non-clinical personnel, however, less so for clinicians. Clinicians are often focused on productivity, because this benefits patients, healthcare facilities and themselves. A transition from 'doing' to 'influence' is required. This requires the development of soft skills in relationship building [5].

This can be challenging for clinicians, as they are accustomed to doing things their way, and to providing orders for patient care on the ward or in the operating room. Building consensus is not typically a skill taught to clinicians or healthcare workers. Learning new skills, and unlearning successful old ones, can be challenging. Clinicians often confuse leadership with management, with the latter having little attraction, as outlined in earlier chapters. One attraction that leadership does hold is the ability to improve the outcomes for patients, including more than one patient at a time [5].

A further barrier for clinicians is that their familiar working environment is highly consistent. In addition, a large proportion of a clinician's identity is tied to his/her clinical work. In the broader complex adaptive system that is healthcare, volatility, uncertainty, risk and ambiguity abound. Spending time in, and training for, the uncertainty of the non-clinical world is therefore highly challenging [5, 6].

The above is a reminder of the importance of involving and training healthcare staff, clinical and non-clinical, in the redesign of healthcare. This empowerment increases engagement and efficiency. Let's look into the mechanics of finding purpose, and of building collaboration into healthcare delivery.

Main Points:

1. Healthcare is at a tipping point, a combination of societal pressures and technology
2. Resistance to change is normal - how we deal with it changes the likelihood of project success
3. Involving all users impacted by change yields creativity benefits, and outcome benefits
4. Digital health is a tool alongside others to reduce complexity - not a magic cure
5. Clinician leadership is vital to champion projects that ultimately benefit many patients

14 FIND PURPOSE IN THE HEALTHCARE EXPERIENCE

'Tell me and I will forget, show me and I may remember, involve me and I will understand.'

Chinese Proverb

Healthcare is about caring. This should be the number one priority for any healthcare provider whether medical, nursing or administrative. Patients want information, and they want to know that we care. When this priority gets subjugated by other 'more important' requirements, the healthcare experience suffers and healthcare outcomes are impaired [1, 2].

REMEMBERING WHY WE ARE HERE

Unfortunately, we see this quite often when patients have 'atypical' questions, or the stress of their situation causes them to focus on peripheral matters. I have seen staff express irritation at having to explain simple processes that are part of their daily routine, forgetting that the patient may never have been through this process before. I have had patients talking at length about their concerns with the air conditioning in the room, rather than wanting to understand more about their anaesthesia or how they will feel post-operatively.

Technological advances have promised change for several decades. However, gains seen in other industries have not translated to healthcare. This is primarily because implementation usually occurs in isolation, according to a perceived simple need. Without regard for the complex interrelationships of healthcare teams and processes, and the needs of the patient, the system becomes broken and the change fails [3].

Bringing together the myriad projects and functions of a healthcare facility is daunting. It is commonly assumed that everyone is there for the same purpose. However, the day-to-day drivers for support staff, clinical staff and managers are markedly different and quickly lead to divergent behaviours. Add to this the maze of external compliance requirements, along with the massive pressures resulting from social and technological changes, and the cracks quickly start to widen. This is where *purpose* becomes the glue.

PURPOSE AND FUNCTION

Note that purpose is not the same as function. The two are commonly confused in healthcare, with 'what we do' often substituted for '*why* we do it'. While performing well at the technical exercise of healthcare delivery would seem a way to unify the enterprise around a common goal, it does not discriminate or define the institution from other similar ones. It also means that individuals, teams and functional units have slightly different performance metrics. Entropy creeps in, with different parts of the organisation pulling in different directions. The opportunity to coordinate the effort of individuals around a common purpose specific to that enterprise is thus lost.

How does an enterprise determine its purpose? Refer to Figure 14 - *Hospital Identity*. Purpose is not simply a generic one, such as 'treating patients'. A specific purpose is informed by the enterprise's identity; its defining and distinguishing values and attributes. These are the 'why' of the enterprise, found after consideration of its history, people, processes and infrastructure. For some, the 'why' relates to a charitable heritage. For others, it may be fulfilling a need in acute care, or palliative care. Within these identities, the facility's market position plays an important role. This may be a focus on the elderly, sports, rehabilitation, neurosurgery, and so forth. Two or three core features will emerge that are distinctive for your facility.

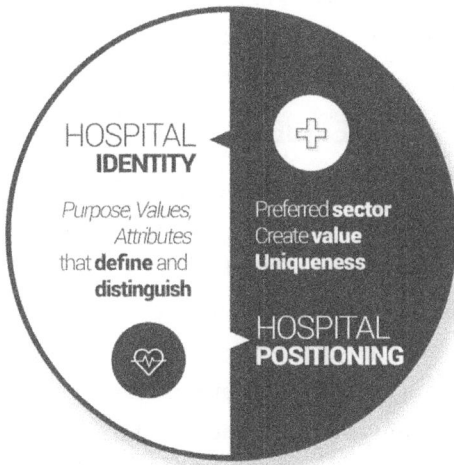

FIGURE 16   A Hospital's Why

These features are then used to generate a short phrase that defines *why* the facility provides the healthcare that it does. This phrase should resonate with all staff, irrespective of their job function. Examples include:

- 'Return to Sport' for a sports-orientated facility,
- 'Active Ageing' for a prehabilitation/rehabilitation facility, or
- 'The Best You' for an integrated primary care clinic.

Purpose is particularly important for the younger generations coming into the workforce, and increasingly important to both employees and consumers. This is where translating the organisation's purpose to local teams and then to individuals comes in. Customising the healthcare facility's 'why' to an individual's tasks is very powerful. It provides purpose in a way that is directly applicable to him or her. In this way, uncertainty is reduced, fear is lessened and resistance to change is minimised [1, 4].

WHY PURPOSE IS THE GLUE

How do we go about this? We need to plan and educate prior to implementation, focusing on the healthcare experience for patients, staff and doctors. Each visiting or employed member of your facility needs to support the 'why', for the whole to be greater than the sum of the parts. For this to occur, both intellectual and emotional engagement needs to happen. This highlights the importance of local context, in considering the effect and responses to an improvement initiative. Combining a required improvement with a locally desired initiative addresses individual and team concerns, assists uptake and supports permanence of the changes [4].

In a similar way, culture can be influenced to support improvements in the safety and quality of the healthcare delivered. Culture is determined by the behaviours, attitudes, beliefs and actions of those within an organisation [1]. Within healthcare organisations, the safety culture has many domains and influences, and is extremely context-sensitive. For many, the question of safety culture change is too difficult an issue, being too big and indistinct to target. However, the process starts with small gains that have a big impact, and progresses to the next project so that (for example) the purpose of 'improving safety is the way that we do healthcare here'.

THE SIX-STEP PROCESS

I recommend a six-step process conducted at the local level, to help gain commitment, increase effort and improve persistence of changes. Please refer to Figure 17 - *Purpose Driven Healthcar*e.

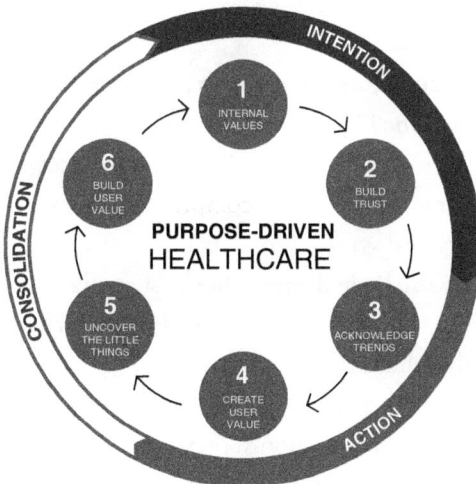

FIGURE 17   Hospital Purpose

1. **Internal values.** A workshop is conducted to map the team's values onto the values of the organisation. This is a useful team building exercise in its own right and has beneficial flow-on effects for individual coaching and career building [4].

2. **Build trust.** Set the stage. Acknowledging team concerns and desires assists in building trust. Ask short, simple, open questions, rather than providing answers. Descriptive ones are preferred, such as 'what's working?', 'what isn't working?', and 'why isn't it working?' This makes it easier to push past biases and dysfunction, and to venture into uncharted territory [4, 5].

3. **Acknowledge trends.** Discuss the external and internal factors leading to the proposed change. Assist brainstorming solutions by asking short, simple, open speculative questions such as 'what if?', 'what might be?', and 'why not?' [4, 5].

4. **Create user value for patients and staff.** At this point you should be in a position to create value by lessening obstacles to performance. Questions are likely to become more cognitively complex, as this stage demands creativity and synthesis of new ideas [5].

5. **Uncover the little things.** Often simple fixes, or those of low perceived value, may be withheld on the mistaken belief that they are not important enough to mention. Many times these apparently trivial items make, or break, projects. Commonly, they will not be volunteered until this late stage of the workshop, as they require considerable individual and team trust [4].

6.   **Build user value.** Whatever change is proposed must be validated against organisational values, and improve the healthcare experience for patients [6] and staff.

Using the above methodology ensures that healthcare is about caring, by and for every healthcare provider. This increases engagement of providers and patients, helping efficiency and quality to improve. Business requirements thus follow clinical requirements. The next chapter examines how a clinician-hospital collaboration vehicle is set up, to meet the requirements of these two pillars of hospital-based healthcare, clinical care and business administration.

MAIN POINTS:

1.   Remember humanity in the patient experience
2.   A good technical outcome is not the same as a good outcome for a patient
3.   Purpose is the personality of an institution, the secret sauce that yields a whole greater than the sum of its parts
4.   A single phrase is essential to encapsulate an organisation's 'Why'
5.   A Six-Step Process is recommended to map institution purpose to local conditions

15 COLLABORATIVE IMPROVEMENT MODEL

'Reward those who Do. Train those who Can't. Replace those who Won't.'

Henn's Creed

How do we resolve the tension between organisational requirements, smooth team functioning and individual meaning or fulfilment in work (and life)? Organisational requirements are set at a board level, without specific reference to individuals. While this is a roadmap of sorts, it doesn't contain the route. It is a recognition of where the organisation is, and where it needs to go, in the broader economic and industry context.

WHO'S DRIVING?

Functional units and teams determine the route that best achieves the organisation's stated goals. As such, teams create change. However, this selection of route doesn't account for local conditions on the road(s) thus travelled. Individuals provide this detail, as does a driver 'on the road'.

A stumbling block is that much of the learning and problem-solving in hospitals occurs in the staff room. This is healthcare's version of the 'water cooler conversations' that occur in office blocks. Interesting medical cases are discussed, near misses and adverse outcomes are dissected, and any perceived shortcomings of hospital administration are analysed. Unfortunately, the administration and clinicians' water coolers are not in the same room, so the two groups come up with unmatched solutions based on half the data/input/creativity available to them.

ARE TWO DRIVERS BETTER THAN ONE?

Training clinicians in leadership seems an obvious course to take. However, clinicians often confuse leadership with management, and management with meetings. Doctors don't like meetings any more than anyone else. They would rather be at the coalface, using their highly trained skills to diagnose and treat patients. The thought of how *best* to deliver healthcare, rather than just delivering it, tends not to come up in a structured way. This is the equivalent of 'working in the business', rather than 'on it', and this compromises improvements in healthcare delivery.

Yet when volunteering on committees for medical associations or hospitals, my business training made it apparent that the goals of good business and good public administration are not that different to the goals of good healthcare:

1. A great customer (patient) experience: placing the customer/patient first;
2. Efficiency: doing the most good with the resources available; and
3. Safety: systems to minimise potential for adverse outcomes.

A common mistake in pursuing healthcare excellence for patients, staff and doctors is to only focus on the clinical aspect, leaving the commercial aspect to look after itself. Improvement 'initiatives' are often built around isolated targets, such as meeting statutory requirements. Business and clinical objectives are assumed at best to be independent, or at worst to compete. However, the reverse is generally true, because good healthcare delivers safer and better clinical outcomes, which are cheaper business outcomes. We are reminded of the social determinants of health, where 80% of healthcare outcomes are driven by non-clinical factors. As a result, many healthcare organisations are leaving value on the table.

HEALTHCARE ORGANISATIONS' MAIN PROBLEMS

Typically, there are three main symptoms in healthcare facilities:

1. Profitability is under constant pressure;
2. The healthcare experience is compromised because of time wasting activities such as duplicated tasks; and
3. Engagement is suboptimal due to the perception that there is no consistent way for patients, staff and doctors to have meaningful input into the healthcare delivery process.

Where there is a healthy relationship between clinical and administrative staff, strong interpersonal relationships drive collaboration (Figure 18). However, there is a high degree of variability in this relationship among healthcare facilities. When this relationship breaks down, the clinical teams and administrative teams each pursue their own agenda. Dysfunctional competition results, with impaired efficiency and quality [1, 2]. We can liken this to cancer, when our own cells pursue their own growth agenda, to the detriment of the body.

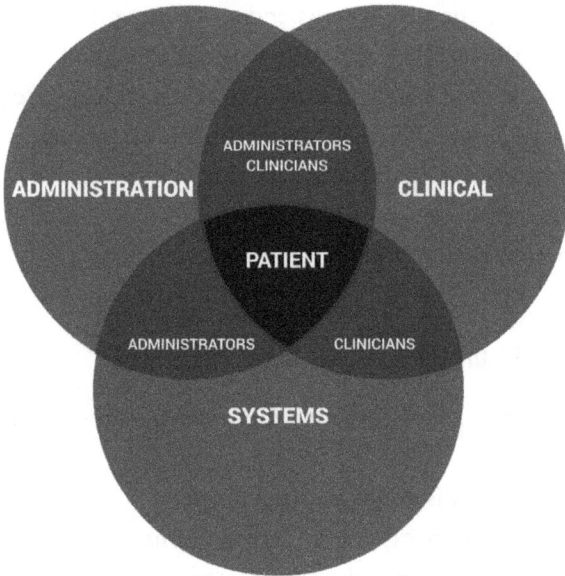

FIGURE 18   Redesign Outcomes

Improving processes and flow of information helps to create better connections between people. Pursuing this collaboration allows for excellence in the healthcare experience, which increases quality and makes the organisation more efficient. Treatments, healthcare providers and timeframes vary, however, the strategies to optimise processes and information flow that reduce cost, reduce risk and improve the experience for patients, nurses and doctors remain the same. How do we diagnose the most important problem to tackle from so many moving parts?

ANOTHER 80:20 SPLIT

This is where collaboration between the clinical and administrative staff demonstrates its value. Because decision-making must be evidence-based, knowledge must be shared so that information can flow freely. Pareto's principle (the '80:20 Rule') reminds us that 80% of the impact will come from 20% of the processes. We need to identify the '20%' - areas ripe for redesign that have a high consumption of resources such as time, people, materials and space. A caveat here is that the likelihood of success for a change project is also an important selection criterion [1, 3].

Often, high cost areas have high variances - variance in cost is often a good surrogate for variation in clinical quality of care [4]. Relevant data is collected to not just identify an area for improvement - the data must also justify the need. For healthcare providers to manage care, they need the right data delivered in the right format at the right time and in the right place. A healthcare enterprise-wide data-warehouse is required to aggregate disparate data from different systems and different care episodes, to provide visibility over clinical and non-clinical costs and outcomes over *relevant* time frames. Often, non-clinical personnel are not in a position to know what time frames are relevant or important [3].

Bear in mind that it is the *care* of the patient that is being managed, not the carers. Cooperation among carers is essential, with care centred around the patient. Transparency in aggregate cost is vital, requiring collaboration from the finance team. This allows the financial impact of proposed care changes to be assessed, to identify where clinical improvements can generate financial savings. It may be that an expensive episode of care is already optimised, or that a variance cannot be meaningfully altered. The level of domain knowledge required means that individual speciality groups must advise on admissions within their own speciality. Lastly, safety must be a property of system redesign. Further reading can be found in The Ten Rules for Redesign, as applicable today as they were in 2001 [5, 6].

CLINICAL-ADMINISTRATIVE COLLABORATION

Synergy occurs when the business side of healthcare (the management and administration systems) works in tandem with the clinical side of healthcare (doctors, nurses and patients). A clinical-administration collaboration entity is required to achieve this state. This entity balances strategy and quality by making decisions informed by all relevant factors. Factors required to achieve this are outlined in Figure 19. Leadership training and mentorship improve strategic thinking skills and decision-making capability. Retaining at least 30% of hours as clinical contact preserves a clinician-executive's credibility with clinical colleagues. The governance structure must accommodate both the broader clinical and administrative bodies' inputs. Compensation must relate in some way to quality of clinical outcomes and patient-reported measures. More than 15% is required to ensure volume-treated is not the primary determinant of behaviour. Compensation can be in-kind, such as improving clinical and administrative infrastructure. This carries the advantage of promoting team-based improvements, and attendant self-regulation, and avoiding perceptions of favouring individuals [2].

COLLABORATIVE IMPROVEMENT MODEL

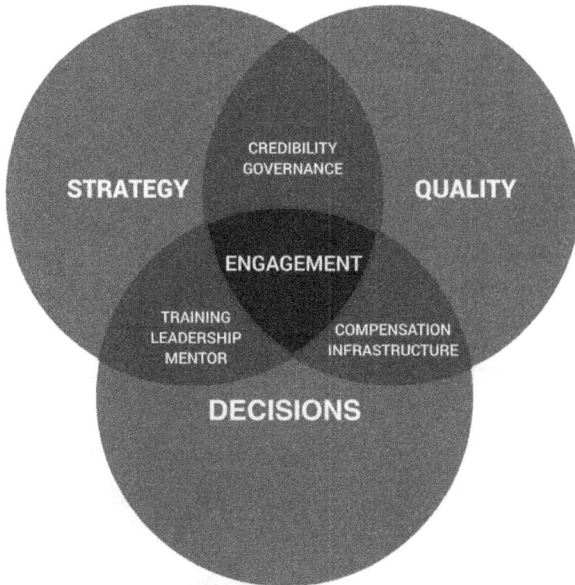

FIGURE 19   Components of A Clinician-Hospital
Collaboration Entity

START SOMEWHERE

For organisations that do not have a healthy relationship between clinical and administrative staff, the first step is to build this relationship. Typically, this is done by starting with a small test project with motivated staff from both areas. A non-contentious improvement project is chosen, such as patient-reported outcome measures, or patient safety. Team prerequisites include having the right leadership capacity for change, and a good team culture. Team consensus on the need for change is important. Project selection will be influenced by having a team willing and able to effect improvement. The change with the highest theoretical payback is not necessarily the most likely to succeed - which would remove any payback at all [2, 3]!

To initiate and foster the process of implementation, and hence support change, a mechanism is required for individuals to provide input and feedback. The simplest mechanism often comes from existing quality incident reporting measures. Extending the familiarity of this process to capturing the healthcare provider experience for clinical staff, and the healthcare delivery experience for patients, closes the feedback loop to help transition the organisational culture into one of 'safety as a way of doing business' (Hudson Stage 5 organisation - Chapter 6) [4].

The icing on the cake after introducing clinical and administrative collaboration is a measurable improvement in staff morale. This is because building collaborative teams tackles complexity, unlike isolated single-issue improvement initiatives. Morale and burnout are big issues in healthcare, across physicians, nurses, pharmacists and allied health care providers. These issues have paralleled the increasing complexity of the industry, with a perception of increasing helplessness on the part of intelligent, highly trained, altruistic healthcare providers [7, 8].

Establishing a clinical collaboration model reinforces values-centred design. Healthcare enterprises that thrive create mutual value, value for the enterprise and value for patients, staff and clinicians. User-led design supports building value. Through involvement of people, your organisation in effect becomes a 'self-learning enterprise'. This positive reinforcement improves engagement and efficiency, and reduces the risk and cost for healthcare enterprises and the healthcare system [8, 9].

MAIN POINTS:

1. Non-clinical drivers of clinical outcomes are more important
2. Construct projects on the drivers that make the most difference
3. First implement projects which are easiest to deliver
4. Clinical Administrative Collaboration is key
5. Start small and build up

16 FUTURE HEALTHCARE

'Those who have knowledge, don't predict. Those who predict, don't have knowledge.'

Lao Tzu

'Prediction is very difficult, especially if it's about the future.'

Niels Bohr

After finding the above quotes, prudence suggested that I abandon this chapter! However, I believe that we have a responsibility to design and create the conditions for an improved world for the next generation. Satisfying this higher purpose is not just the 'right thing to do' - it provides personal fulfilment. My life experiences and learnings lead me to see a future healthcare that is exquisitely tailored to the individual, to optimise health quality throughout one's life span. So it adds life to years, not just years to life. It also adds productivity to society – healthcare becomes an investment, rather than a tax.

'The best way to predict the future is to create it.'

Peter Drucker

How can this come about? Hopefully by now you will see the importance of aligning incentives between the clinical world and the business of healthcare. You will have seen that financial and clinical transparency, in context, is possible, desirable and inevitable. You will also see the importance of taking the lead and informing the conversation in order to improve healthcare and benefit our patients.

A convergence of technologies is increasing the depth of expertise of healthcare that can be made available at every interaction. These technologies are also enabling a greater breadth of delivery, so that healthcare is available inexpensively to more people in more places at more times. Healthcare is becoming more accessible, available and affordable for everyone. I summarise many of these *existing* technologies below.

CONNECTEDNESS

We are familiar with the Internet, delivered via satellite, wires and wirelessly. For mobile applications this is about to become significantly faster with the '5G' standard being rolled out in 2019. For healthcare, this means rapid transmission of very large data files, such as diagnostic imaging, can become widely available with less need for dedicated infrastructure [1].

This further supports interoperability and exchange of health information to support transitions of care. As interoperability becomes more sophisticated, the sending and receiving systems know not just where to put the information, but what to do with it as well. Faster connections are also an important prerequisite for the explosion of devices able to be connected to the Internet, the so-called Internet of Things (IoT). Increasingly, this means *anything* able to convey an electrical current [2].

BLOCKCHAIN

Essentially, this is a way of securing transactions between parties without a third agent being required to identify the parties. Changing any transactions in any block alters the signatures and makes tampering immediately evident. Applications include drug, device and implant traceability; authentication and interoperability of health records and data; smart contracts; clinical trials; genomics research and precision medicine. Not having a third agent reduces the cost of transactions and increases the speed. It allows an individual to share their genomic or other personal data, to keep track of where it goes and potentially sell their own data – without the recipient knowing who it has come from, or worse, a third party selling it without the knowledge or consent of the original individual [2, 3].

WEARABLE SENSORS

With nanotechnology, measurements can be taken non-invasively from wearable items such as contacts and clothing. Jewellery can contain sensors, and home test kits can analyse body secretions such as exhaled breath, waste and sweat. This leads to the concept of the 'digital exhaust' and a 'body dashboard' with early warning lights, much as we take for granted in our vehicles [4].

Existing internal and optional attachable sensors can provide similar functionality from mobile phones. Cranial sensors behind the ear can interpret emotion and wirelessly transmit this to a smart phone or local network for use in, and monitoring of, therapy. [5]

ARTIFICIAL INTELLIGENCE (AI)

AI can be applied at a lower level (machine learning) to look for changes in an individual's digital exhaust that may indicate disease. Repetitive tasks, such as reading medical imaging and pathology slides, lend themselves well to the use of machine learning, by flagging exceptions. AI doesn't sleep and doesn't forget.

AI can also be applied at a high level to learn and analyse movement patterns, digital device usage patterns, such as social media content, voice tone and speaking patterns, and facial expressions. This becomes a higher mental function dashboard to combine with the body dashboard for even more finely-tuned personalised analytics. With this integration of multiple sources of information, psychological distress and biological disease can be detected earlier. Awareness of the precursors of ill health increases, and the stigma of seeking help decreases [6]. Interestingly, humans are more revealing and spend up to twice as long with an AI therapist, compared to a human one [5]. Perhaps this is because we know the AI doesn't get bored, isn't judgemental and doesn't cost by the minute!

Yiersly, an expert in the field, equates current AI intelligence with the level of a chimpanzee. [5] However, AI learns as it learns, meaning its ability to make assumptions and test solutions from raw data is increasing rapidly. It is possible in a year or two that AI intelligence will rival an uneducated human, and rival Einstein a few years after that. Humans (or robots) are required to enable AI to perform physical functions, so for the medium term it would seem its role is to support human undertakings.

Nonetheless, we are on the edge of a change apparently comparable to the rise of human life on earth that will therefore alter the future of humanity, without fully knowing what the implications will be, and with an unknown time to understand and address those implications [7].

BIG DATA

The volume and speed with which data collects is staggering. In addition to the above biometric and machine data, other sources include the web and social media, financial transactions, human-generated data, such as medical records and communications, and pharmaceutical/therapeutic goods data. This data already exists, however, we are not making use of it in healthcare. Special techniques are required to collect and aggregate the data in ways that it can be usefully analysed and subsequently applied to improve patient care, decisions, clinical trials, and business outcomes [2].

HEALTH AND WELLNESS APPS

These put awareness, education and early intervention in the hands of patients/consumers. Typical functions include prescription and appointment management, medical reference, health and wellness promotion and remote patient monitoring. Gamification is used to increase enjoyment of usage and hence compliance with treatment. As the quality of AI interpretation of collected data increases, the lines between consumer products and regulated medical applications that diagnose and treat diseases are becoming blurred [2].

ROBOTICS

Applications include lab assistant robots, soft and hard exoskeletons for rehabilitation and mobility, soft cardiac pouch pumps for heart failure, microrobotics for equipment inspections and nanorobots for delivering medication or other payloads internally. Robots are already working alongside humans in pharmacies and laboratories. Society needs to grapple with the implications of provision of autonomy to robotics [7].

REMOTE INTERACTIONS

Improving the user experience when interacting with technology makes use of gesture, voice, movement, gaze or other Natural User Interface (NUI) techniques. This can happen locally or remotely, meaning that telehealth can be performed with natural inputs and feedback for both clinician and patient, for diagnosis, learning, rehabilitation and social interactions. See the Microsoft Research Centre for Social Natural User Interfaces at the University of Melbourne [8].

AUGMENTED AND VIRTUAL REALITY

Virtual reality combines human senses with software and hardware to enable real time interaction with a 3-D computer generated environment. Typical equipment required includes headsets for sound and vision and to exclude the real world, special gloves for spatial detection and feedback, and even treadmills for movement. Augmented reality is the superimposition of virtual reality on the real world, either through projection on to real objects, specialised eye glasses (Google Glass, Microsoft HoloLens) or viewing through a smart phone or tablet. Both AR and VR are used for medical learning, remote supervision, and remote therapeutics in the home, community or hospital [2].

ORGANS AND IMPLANTS

Drugs, devices, and implants are already being 3-D printed, enabling customisation anywhere, anytime. Current devices print in two dimensions, layering to create the third dimension over an hour or two. The next generation of devices are able to form complete complex 3-D structures, by projecting a hologram into a formative soup, with much more precision and much shorter time frames (seconds). These technologies mean that any therapeutic agent or device can be sent electronically anywhere, once power and a printer are available. In combination with solar cells and drones, advanced therapeutics can be made available in remote areas without expensive expenditure on road and electricity infrastructure [4].

GENOMICS

As genome mapping has fallen in cost from millions to hundreds of dollars, gene modification techniques have also developed. For reprogramming DNA, whether to remove inherited genetic disease or, in effect, to create stem cells, or to recognise and destroy cancer cells Clustered Regularly Interspaced Short Palindromic Repeats (CRISPR) gene-editing technology is used, originally discovered from a bacterial defence system against viral attacks. Reprogramming immunity with chimeric antigen receptor T-cell Therapy (CAR-T) is showing promise for cancer treatment. Reprogramming cells can be achieved with somatic cell nuclear transfer (SCNT) to create a viable embryo from a body cell and an enucleated egg cell – in effect a clone. From cartilage replacement to organs, grown in host animals using the patient's tissue, the applications are extensive [3].

ETHICS

Healthcare data is rich in identifiers used for identity and financial theft, leading to increasing hacker attacks. When everyone is a patient at one time or another, security is paramount. With so many connected devices, we must ensure they are not hacked and/or ransomed to avoid a pacemaker being turned off, identities being stolen, or a hospital or health record system being blocked [9].

Advanced medical therapies carry a danger of widening the socioeconomic gap, by creating physically and intellectually advanced individuals. Advanced technology similarly can widen the gap if access is unequal. Convergence of the above technologies creates extraordinary opportunities. Artificial intelligence will accelerate the learnings in all disciplines. Like any new idea or device their use can create harm or benefit. Robust frameworks, discussion by society and feedback is critical to ensure we design a future, and healthcare future, that we want to live in.

So what future would you like to design? Much proactive and personalised healthcare will occur outside of traditional existing healthcare delivery structures. However, rather than threatening the existence of traditional healthcare providers,

I believe this will lead to a fundamental redesign of the way healthcare is delivered – from reactive to proactive, from generic to highly personalised, from reactive disease-care to lifelong health optimisation. This means the availability of healthcare far beyond its traditional time, money, logistic and staffing limits to encompass theoretically everyone, everywhere, all the time. Without the wide and inexpensive reach of technology this would not be possible. Our biggest problems are our biggest opportunities.

Main Points:

1. We have a responsibility to create future healthcare - and society
2. Healthcare adds life to individuals and productivity to society
3. Connected, secure, personalised data permits predictive analytics
4. Machine learning and AI are able to utilise enormous volumes of data
5. Breaking geographic, informational, supply and time limitations permits 24/7 healthcare anywhere, anytime for everyone

CONCLUSION

'Start with short stories. After all, if you were taking up rock climbing, you wouldn't start with Mount Everest.'

George R. R. Martin

In closing, an irony to me is that Peter Drucker's holistic approach to management was born of necessity and drew on a medical analogy. When starting as a management consultant in the 1940s, he found incomplete guidance. There were books on individual aspects of operating a business, such as finance or human resources, but there was nothing that connected all of the parts to provide context. To Drucker, this would be like producing a book on human anatomy that discussed one joint in isolation, without mentioning the limb, let alone the skeleton and musculature. He remedied this by writing *The Practice of Management* [1].

Today, we find ourselves in a similar situation, where the business and clinical halves of the healthcare brain do not communicate effectively. Worse, this is compounded by the various systems within these halves being siloed from one another. Where to from here? How do you plan to get more control in your work, more enjoyment and better results for your efforts? A suggested approach is outlined below, and more tools can be found at www.douglasfahlbusch.com.

1.   CLARITY OF PURPOSE

Set aside an hour a week just for you. This island of time enables you to reflect on your purpose, e.g. improving the patient experience, or better work-life integration. Why did you originally get into healthcare? Does this still apply? For me, it is now 'Reimagining healthcare to ensure accessibility, availability and affordability for everyone'.

This time also enables you to identify the main problems or obstacles that you currently face, in order to efficiently tackle them. Remember, the biggest obstacles and constraints provide the biggest opportunities. Consider:

- **Last week:** Did I move towards my purpose? What worked? What didn't?
- **This week:** What will you do at work and at home to move a step closer to achieving your purpose?

2.   ROUTINE

Structure frees your efforts, by ensuring routine tasks are completed 'by default' in the normal course of events. A suggested format is:

- **Daily:** meet with your team to discuss its purpose, and its actions. What are/were the highs, lows and actions being held up. Most teams do this at the start of the day.
- **Weekly:** meet with your peers to discuss processes and systems. This is an important step in uncovering workarounds, where a better system or process would remove the need for the workaround.

- **Monthly:** meet with peers to discuss actual progress against planned progress, allocating resources where most required.
- **Quarterly:** A strategic meeting, where wins and misses against the purpose are analysed, and an outline is then set for the next quarter.

In our crazy-busy work and personal lives, a daily reminder of what you are trying to achieve is warranted. For some, this reminder is most effective on rising. For others, it is more effective at the end of the day. A suggested format is:

- **Yesterday's Goal or Task:** Was this achieved? What worked? What didn't?
- **Today's Goal:** It is helpful to have one over-riding goal each day that moves towards your purpose, amongst the myriad of tasks that require daily attention.

3. SKILLS

Developing these helps you, your patients and your practice or hospital. The types of skills that are useful include:

- **Clinical Leadership:** Communication, Empathy, Influence, Negotiation, Collaboration, Engagement, Leading and Aligning teams, Conflict resolution, Leading change, Research
- **Strategy:** Creativity/Innovation, Identifying Constraints, Strengths, Weaknesses, Trends, Threats, Opportunities, Prioritisation, Values
- **Governance:** Quality, Reliability, Hospital-/ Practice-Clinician Integration, Health and Medical Law, Population Health, Disaster Planning, Ethics

- **Management:** Finance, Accounting, Resource Allocation, Business Plans, Team Performance, Project and Change Management, Data, Internal and External Customers, Patient-Reported Outcome Measures, Training

A number of service providers target specific areas. Feel free to use our diagnostic tool at www.douglasfahlbusch.com to see which area would be most productive for you to focus on. Or contact us to discuss our online and in-person courses that are a broad-brush approach to fill in the gaps. It's a great way to take stock and decide where to go next with your career.

4.   DESIGN YOUR FUTURE

What do you want the next phase of your career to look like? Consider trends such as social, technological, medico-legal, regulatory, research, economic, political and environmental.

- **Examine What Works Elsewhere** – and what doesn't. Some examples are included below.
- **Systems Thinking:** Increase the chances of a successful outcome, while simultaneously decreasing the chances of unwanted effects.
- **User Experience:** Improving the healthcare experience for patients and providers increases success. Patient-reported outcome measures form the common glue for improvement interventions. Everyone can get on board with things that matter to patients – and if they don't, you should question their commitment and fit to your organisation's purpose.

- **Healthcare not Disease-Care:** Social determinants of health and the above two measures will help you to reimagine your delivery of healthcare – and ultimately that of the community, state and country.

5. TOOLS FOR IMPLEMENTATION.

- **Responsible Marketing**, including social media. See the case example below.
- **Co-Design:** Asking 'What matters to you?' is important for both patients and healthcare personnel. Frameworks are available from www.IHI.org and www.ICHOM.org
- **Project Design and Management.** A variety of methodologies are available. Selection will depend on local expertise and culture.
- **Motivation and Management of Teams.** Again, a variety of tools are available, and selection comes from local relevance. Implementation is aided by demonstrating the value of clinician leadership, through local examples of improved patient and care-team outcomes. Circulation of clinical performance assists engagement with the non-clinical system aspects of care improvement.
- **Use of Technology and Data.** Partner with experts that meet your design criteria – don't be told what to do.

CASE EXAMPLES

Marketing and Social Media. Online platforms enable a 24/7 presence via the use of online information, videos, questionnaires and downloads. The cost of creating these is quickly offset through reduced staff time for repetitive questions or basic education. Patients and staff can access these materials at a time and place of convenience or relevance.

'Social' media is two-way – the reader or user is able to interact with the medium. Healthcare often hesitates to provide patients and staff with the ability to post information online. Moderation of comments is recommended to ensure confidentiality is maintained. Daily monitoring is required to respond to feedback or requests for information, not just from the healthcare facility's web presence, but from a plethora of online forums. Automatic search term alerts such as Google Alerts are recommended, to notify the facility when it is mentioned in posts.

CODESIGN

Workflow mapping is done most quickly and simply with post-it notes on a white board, facilitated by a coach or manager. In this way all participants can identify the steps that they complete, write the steps on postop notes, uncover duplication and organise the steps into their workflow(s) on the whiteboard. This process typically takes sixty minutes, and is faster when participants come prepared with a list of frequently asked questions.

Two experienced observers should take notes, to minimise misconceptions and missed detail. Steps unknown to some, or taken for granted and not spelt out, are identified in this way. An electronic version of the workflow is then created, and updated to correct any errors or missing information, such as missing team members' tasks. Next, a real-time follow-through in the workplace provides an initial validation of the workflow.

The team then reconvenes to verify and simplify the workflow. e.g.

1. Identify Gaps,
2. Find Value Adds, and
3. Understand and Document causes of process variances.

This brings reality to the concepts, and ensures that high value improvements are targeted, instead of change for the sake of change. When multiple opportunities are identified, start with one that has the team best-positioned to follow through with the improvement. Note that this is not necessarily the highest value improvement – often a 'quick win' with a lesser value improvement builds momentum and persistence for more difficult, higher value changes.

PRE-ADMISSION WORKFLOWS

A 300 bed hospital was experiencing increasing acuity of patients, due to more sophisticated operating theatre equipment and intensive care facilities that permitted a wider range of surgeries and management of more serious patient diseases. Allocation of in-hospital resources was occurring on the day of admission, leading to unnecessary cost and potential risk, with expensive and time-consuming workarounds ('fire-fighting'). Preparatory interviews identified several high-value steps in the pre-admission workflow from community to hospital. A half-day session followed, at which the steps were prioritised according to ease of implementation. A step that would be simple to implement was chosen to ease the workload for team members.

By creating this early 'win', team commitment to more complex stages was generated. The ongoing benefit of 'working smarter, not harder' reduced staff time costs, improved efficiency and morale, and reduced resource consumption, such as repeating investigations or unplanned high acuity ward allocations.

'SIMPLEX MANAGEMENT'

A 350 bed hospital wanted to differentiate its operating theatre equipment. Large high definition screens were chosen as a feature for surgeons. However, the supplier selected did not provide compatibility with existing cabling and infrastructure. Consequently, new stand-alone placement and cabling was installed. However, the ergonomics were inferior, causing surgeon fatigue, and occupational health and safety risks to staff. Theatre throughput was slowed, from both increased physical movements of equipment, and through team impairment following indifference from management to feedback provided by the team.

The recommended approach of a limited physical trial with rapid (weekly or fortnightly) feedback and improvement iterations was not taken. This systems-based approach would have promptly uncovered the unintended consequences outlined above, allowing a more considered approach to device selection. This approach would have reduced direct costs, such as increased labour time, and indirect costs, such as impaired morale.

I hope the need for change is clear, that your frustration with our current 'disease-care' system can now have an outlet, and that some methods to improve or change the system are begging to be trialled. Please consider this broader application of healthcare as a form of health advocacy by physicians. I believe that we should advocate for social, economic, educational, and political changes that ameliorate suffering and contribute to human well-being, especially in this time of change that has no precedence in human history for its scale or speed.

Main Points:

1. Dedicate time for clarity in purpose
2. Set routines to set your time and energy free
3. Develop leadership skills
4. Learn tools for implementation
5. Help design the future

REFERENCES

Introduction

1. Chase, D., *CEO's Guide to Restoring the American Dream*. 2017, Bellingham, WA, USA: Health Rosetta Media. 279.
2. Shen, L. and S. Decarlo. *Microsoft Becomes Second Most Valuable Company For First Time Since 2015*. Fortune Magazine, 2018. http://fortune.com/2018/04/24/microsoft-becomes-second-most-valuable-company-for-first-time-since-2015/
3. Martin, B. *Corporatisation of Healthcare*. 2007; Available from: http://www.bmartin.cc/dissent/documents/health/map_australia.html.

Chapter 1

1. Frost, J., *Five Health Stocks to Improve Your Vital Signs*, in *Australian Financial Review*. 2015.
2. Chase, D., *CEO's Guide To Restoring The American Dream*. 2017, Bellingham, WA, USA: Health Rosetta Media. 279.
3. Chase, D. *Healthcare Disruption: Pharma 3.0 Will Drive Shift from Life Science to HealthTech Investing (Part I of III)*. TechCrunch, 2011.
4. Institute, G., *Health is the biggest pressure on government budgets overall*. 2014, Grattan Institute.
5. AIHW *Australia's hospitals 2015–16*. 2017.
6. ABS. *6333.0 - Characteristics of Employment, Australia, August 2016*. [document] 2017 2017-05-02 [cited 2017 DEC2017]; Available from: http://www.abs.gov.au/ausstats/abs@.nsf/Latestproducts/6333.0Main%20Features2August%202016?opendocument&tabname=Summary&prodno=6333.0&issue=August%202016&num=&view=.
7. CommonwealthFund. *International Health Care System Profiles*. 2016; Available from: http://international.commonwealthfund.org/.

8.   Sisodia, R.S., Jagdish N.; Wolfe, David, *Firms of Endearment: How World-Class Companies Profit from Passion and Purpose (2nd Edition)* 2ed. 2014, USA.

9.   Sikka, R., J.M. Morath, and L. Leape, *The Quadruple Aim: care, health, cost and meaning in work.* 2015.

10.   Plsek, P.E., *The challenge of complexity in health care.* 2001, BMJ.

11.   WHO *Systems Thinking for Health Systems Strengthening.* 2009.

12.   Hudson, P., *Applying the lessons of high risk industries to health care.* 2003.

13.   Britnell, M., *In Search of the Perfect Health System.* 2015: Palgrave Macmillan. Kindle Edition.

14.   Ageing, Australian Government Department of Health and Ageing. *Chronic Conditions.* 2017. DOI: http://www.health.gov.au/internet/main/publishing.nsf/Content/chronic-disease.

15.   Institute, G., *A vision for creating a healthy Australia.* 2017.

16.   Porter, M.E.H., James E., *Why Every Organization Needs an Augmented Reality Strategy.* Harvard Business Review, 2017. 95(6): p. 11.

17.   Weber, D.O. *Artificial Intelligence Is a Growing Force in Health Care.* Hospital & Health Networks, 2015.

18.   Morse, G., *One Company's Experience with AR.* Harvard Business Review, 2017. 95(6): p. 2.

19.   Byers, J. and S. Muchmore *The healthcare of tomorrow will move away from hospitals.* HealthDIVE, 2017.

20.   Smith, P. *Lean Health Care Interview with Virginia Mason Medical Center.* 2017.

Chapter 2

1.   Kuipers, P., Kendall, E., Ehrlich, C., McIntyre, M., Barber, L., Amsters, D., Kendall, M., Kuipers, K., Muenchberger, H. & Brownie, S. *Complexity and health care: health practitioner workforce services, roles, skills and training, to respond to patients with complex needs.* 2011 [cited

2017; Available from: https://www.health.qld.gov.au/__data/assets/ pdf_file/0027/150768/complexcarefull1.pdf.

2. Plsek, P.E., *The challenge of complexity in health care*. 2001, BMJ.

3. Safford, M.M., J.J. Allison, and C.I. Kiefe, *Patient Complexity: More Than Comorbidity. The Vector Model of Complexity | SpringerLink*. Journal of General Internal Medicine, 2007. 22(Supplement 3): p. 382–390.

4. Britnell, M., *In Search of the Perfect Health System*. 2015: Palgrave Macmillan. Kindle Edition.

5. Schleiter, K.E., *Difficult Patient-Physician Relationships and the Risk of Medical Malpractice Litigation, Mar 09 ... Virtual Mentor*. AMA Journal of Ethics, 2009. 11(3): p. 242-246.

6. Sohn, D.H., *Negligence, genuine error, and litigation*, in *Int J Gen Med*. 2013. p. 49-56.

7. Studdert, D.M., et al., *Relationship between Quality of Care and Negligence Litigation in Nursing Homes*. NEJM, 2011. 364(March): p. 1243-50.

8. Stelfox, H.T., et al., *The relation of patient satisfaction with complaints against physicians and malpractice lawsuits*. Am J Med, 2005. 118(10): p. 1126-33.

9. Andel, C., et al., *The economics of health care quality and medical errors*. J Health Care Finance, 2012. 39(1): p. 39-50.

10. Care, Australian Commission on Safety and Quality in Healthcare, *Entity Resources and Planned Performance*, H.P. Entity, Editor. 2016.

11. Glover, L. *The Australian Health Care System*. International Health Care System Profiles 2016 [cited 2017; Available from: http:// international.commonwealthfund.org/countries/australia/.

12. Roughhead, L.S., S; Rosenfeld, E, *Literature Review: Medication Safety in Australia (2013)*. Australian Commission on Safety and Quality in Healthcare. Care, Editor. 2013, Australian Government: Sydney.

13. AIHW, *Trends in injury deaths, Australia 1999–00 to 2011–12*, Australian Institute of Health and Welfare. Welfare, Editor. 2017, Australian Government.

14. Makary, M.A. and M. Daniel, *Medical error—the third leading cause of death in the US.* BMJ, 2016. 353.

15. Russo, P.L., et al., *Healthcare-associated infections in Australia: time for national surveillance.* Australian Health Review, 2017. **39**(1): p. 37-43.

16. Worth, L.J., et al., *Diminishing surgical site infections in Australia: time trends in infection rates, pathogens and antimicrobial resistance using a comprehensive Victorian surveillance program, 2002-2013.* Infect Control Hosp Epidemiol, 2015. 36(4): p. 409-16.

17. AIHW, *Approached to Surgical Site Infection Surveillance For acute care settings in Australia,* Australian Commission on Safety and Quality in Healthcare. Care. Care, Editor. 2017, Australian Government.

18. Wilson, R.M., et al., *The Quality in Australian Health Care Study.* Med J Aust, 1995. 163(9): p. 458-71.

19. Australian Bureau of Statistics, *Coordination of health care.* 2017, Commonwealth of Australia.

20. Nikhil R. SahniAnuraag ChigurupatiBob Kocher, M.M.C., *How the U.S. Can Reduce Waste in Health Care Spending by $1 Trillion.* HBR, 2015.

21. Organisation for Economic Co-operation and Development. *Tackling Wasteful Spending on Health.* 2017; Available from: https://www.oecd.org/els/health-systems/Tackling-Wasteful-Spending-on-Health-Highlights-revised.pdf.

22. Creighton A, T.S., *Healthcare waste costs $20bn a year,* in *The Weekend Australian.* 2016, News Corp: Australia.

23. Wolfe, A., *Institute of Medicine Report: Crossing the Quality Chasm: A New Health Care System for the 21st Century.* http://dx.doi.org/10.1177/152715440100200312, 2016.

24. Garrett, J., *Effective Perioperative Communication to Enhance Patient Care- ClinicalKey.* AORN, 2016. 104(2): p. 111-120.

25. ABS, *Patient Experiences in Australia: Summary of Findings, 2016-17,* Australian Bureau of Statistics, Editor. 2017, Commonwealth of Australia.

Chapter 3

1.   Ashkenas, R., *Change Management Needs to Change.* Harvard Business Review, 2013.

2.   *Drucker Institute Company Rankings: Background.* 2017; Available from: http://www.drucker.institute/rankings-background/.

3.   Roman, J.K. *Solving the Wrong Pockets Problem.* 2017.

4.   RitzCarlton, L., *Patient Experience Impacts Safety* 2015, The Ritz-Carlton. p. When healthcare organizations become more patient-centric they empower employees and increase engagement, improve the patient experience and improve safety saving lives.

5.   Mayes, L., *Beyond the Stethoscope: Doctors' stories of reclaiming hope, heart and healing in medicine.* 2017: www.lucymayes.com.

Chapter 4

1.   Mayes, L., *Beyond the Stethoscope: Doctors' stories of reclaiming hope, heart and healing in medicine.* 2017: www.lucymayes.com.

2.   Gawande, A., *The Checklist Manifesto.* 2009.

3.   Roman, J.K. *Solving the Wrong Pockets Problem.* 2017.

4.   Editorial, *The New Marketplace of Health Care - Impacts and Incentives of Payment Reform.* NEJM, 2017.

5.   Arnold, R.D. and J.P. Wade, *A Definition of Systems Thinking: A Systems Approach.* Procedia Computer Science, 2015. 44(Supplement C): p. 669-678.

6.   Serino, M., *Quality and Patient Safety Teams in the Perioperative Setting- ClinicalKey.* AORN Journal, 2015-12-01. 102(6): p. 617-628.

7.   Kaplan, G. and C. Stokes. *Leading a Culture of Safety: A Blueprint for Success.* 2017; Available from: http://www.ache.org/pdf/secure/Leading_a_Culture_IHI_7-25-17.pdf.

8.   Hudson, P., *Applying the lessons of high risk industries to health care.* 2003.

9.   Walker, B. and S.A. Soule, *Changing Company Culture Requires a Movement, Not a Mandate.* HBR, 2017.

10. Sinek, S. *Transform Culture*. 2017; Available from: https://startwithwhy.com/transform-culture/.

11. ACHE. *Top Issues Confronting Hospitals*. 2016; Available from: http://www.ache.org/pubs/research/ceoissues.cfm.

12. Smart, G., *Who: the A method for hiring*. 2008, USA: Ballantine Books.

13. ACSQHC. *National Priorities*. 2017; Available from: https://www.safetyandquality.gov.au/national-priorities/.

14. AIHW, *Trends in injury deaths, Australia 1999–00 to 2011–12*, Australian Institue of Health and Welfare, Editor. 2017, Australian Government.

15. ACSQHC. *Clinical Handover*. 2017; Available from: https://www.safetyandquality.gov.au/our-work/clinical-communications/clinical-handover/.

16. Agarwala, A., S. Nurudeen, and A. Haynes, *Perioperative Checklists and Handoffs*. Advances in Anesthesia, 2015. 33(1): p. 191-217.

17. America, Committee on Quality of Health Care in America, *To Err Is Human/ Building a Safer Health System*, ed. Institute of Medicine. 2000.

18. Britnell, M., *In Search of the Perfect Health System*. 2015: Palgrave Macmillan. Kindle Edition.

19. Mitchell, K. *Like Magic? ("Every system is perfectly designed...")*. 2015.

20. HealthTap. *HealthTap - Ask doctors now and get immediate help for free 24/7 - Advice, prescriptions, reminders, and more*. 2017.

21. Pontious, M.J., *Understanding the "Worried Well"*. The Journal of Family Practice, 2002. 51(1).

Chapter 5

1. Coulter, I.D. and E.M. Willis, *The rise and rise of complementary and alternative medicine: a sociological perspective*. The Medical Journal of Australia, 2018. 180(11): p. 587-589.

2. Clarke, T.C., et al., *Trends in the use of complementary health approaches*

among adults: United States, 2002-2012. Natl Health Stat Report, 2015(79): p. 1-16.

3.   Olson, K.D., *Physician Burnout—A Leading Indicator of Health System Performance? - Mayo Clinic Proceedings.* Mayo Clinic Proceedings, 2017. 92(11): p. 3.

4.   beyondblue *National Mental Health Survey of Doctors and Medical Students.* 2018.

5.   Holland, P. and T.L. Tham *Burnt-out and overworked, Australia's nurses and midwives consider leaving profession.* 2016.

6.   Shanafelt, T.D., et al., *Longitudinal Study Evaluating the Association Between Physician Burnout and Changes in Professional Work Effort - Mayo Clinic Proceedings.* Mayo Clinic Proceedings, 2016. 91(4): p. 9.

7.   CDC. *Suicide: Risk and Protective Factors.* 2017 2017-10-03T03:00:17Z; Available from: https://www.cdc.gov/violenceprevention/suicide/riskprotectivefactors.html.

8.   Gawande, A., *The Checklist Manifesto.* 2009.

9.   Sikka, R., J.M. Morath, and L. Leape, *The Quadruple Aim: care, health, cost and meaning in work.* 2015.

10. Institute for Healthcare Improvement. *Quality Improvement Essentials Toolkit.* 2017; Available from: http://www.ihi.org/resources/Pages/Tools/Quality-Improvement-Essentials-Toolkit.aspx.

Chapter 6

1.   Britnell, M., *In Search of the Perfect Health System.* 2015: Palgrave Macmillan. Kindle Edition.

2.   OECD. *Tackling Wasteful Spending on Health.* 2017; Available from: https://www.oecd.org/els/health-systems/Tackling-Wasteful-Spending-on-Health-Highlights-revised.pdf.

3.   Nikhil R. SahniAnuraag ChigurupatiBob Kocher, M.M.C., *How the U.S. Can Reduce Waste in Health Care Spending by $1 Trillion.* HBR, 2015.

4.   Creighton A, T.S., *Healthcare waste costs $20bn a year*, in *The Weekend Australian*. 2016, News Corp: Australia.

5.   Hudson, P., *Applying the lessons of high risk industries to health care*. 2003.

6.   Gawande, A., *The Checklist Manifesto*. 2009.

7.   World Health Organisation, *WHO surgical safety checklist and implementation manual*. Safe Surgery Saves Lives 2010 2010-12-08 22:19:00 11 Jan 18]; Available from: http://www.who.int/patientsafety/safesurgery/ss_checklist/en/.

8.   Institute, C.I., *Successful Delivery of Mega-Projects*, in *2015 Construction Industry Institute Annual Conference*, R.T. 315, Editor. 2015, The University of Texas at Austin.

9.   Manchanda, R., *What Is an "Upstreamist" in Health Care?* 2016, Institute for Healthcare Improvement.

10. World Health Organisation, *Systems Thinking for Health Systems Strengthening*. 2009.

11. Lindsey, K.R.W.J.S., *Engage and Align with Physicians*, in *Take Charge of Your Healthcare Management Career: 50 Lessons that Drive Success*, A. Baumann, Editor. 2015, Association of University Programs in Health Administration, Health Administration Press: Chicago, Illinois. p. 4.

Chapter 7

1.   Smith, M., et al., *Engaging Patients, Families, and Communities*, in *Best Care at Lower Cost: The Path to Continuously Learning Health Care in America.*, Committee on the Learning Health Care System in America, Editor. 2013, National Academies Press (US).

2.   Smith, P. *Lean Health Care Interview with Virginia Mason Medical Center*. 2017.

3.   Joseph Dwyer, S.J., and Sylvia Vriesendorp, *Occasional Paper: An Urgent Call to Professionalize Leadership and Management Health Care Worldwide*. Management Sciences for Health, 2006. 4: p. 31.

4. Duncan, E.N., and Sarah Tucker-Ray, *Avoiding the seven deadly sins of customer-experience transformations.* 2017.

5. DiJulius, J., *The Customer Service Revolution: Overthrow Conventional Business, Inspire Employees, and Change the World.* 2015, Austin, Texas, USA: Greenleaf Book Group.

6. Gleeson, H., et al., *Systematic review of approaches to using patient experience data for quality improvement in healthcare settings.* BMJ Open, 2016. 6(8).

7. PressGaneyAssociates *Total Patient Experience, Not Just Satisfaction Scores, Tied to Quality.* PG Snapshot, 2017. 16.

8. RitzCarlton, L., *Patient Experience Impacts Safety* 2015, The Ritz-Carlton. p. When healthcare organizations become more patient-centric they empower employees and increase engagement, improve the patient experience and improve safety saving lives.

9. Solomon, M. *Improve The Patient Experience By Consulting Models Outside of Healthcare.* Forbes, 2014.

10. Ayala, D.M.L. *The Root of All Satisfaction - Patients Want Caregivers Who Provide Information and Compassion.* PG Snapshot, 2017.

11. Solomon, M. *9 Patient Experience And Satisfaction Secrets For Hospitals And Healthcare.* Forbes, 2014.

12. Torpie, K., *Customer service vs. Patient care.* Patient Experience Journal, 2014. 1(2): p. 3.

13. Elbert, N.J., et al., *Effectiveness and cost-effectiveness of ehealth interventions in somatic diseases: a systematic review of systematic reviews and meta-analyses.* J Med Internet Res, 2014. 16(4): p. e110.

14. Balster, J. *How to make creative collaboration work.* Creative Review, 2016.

15. Dylan Minor; Brook, P.B., Josh, *Data From 3.5 Million Employees Shows How Innovation Really Works.* Harvard Business Review, 2017.

16. CHC. *Conference for Health Care.* 2017; Available from: http://chc-qms.com/en/.

17. Virginia Mason Institute. *Lean Health Care Improvement.* 2018; Available from: https://www.virginiamasoninstitute.org/.

Chapter 8

1.   Haughom, J., *Quality Improvement in Healthcare: 5 Deming Principles*. 2016.

2.   Kaissi, A., *Enhancing physician engagement: an international perspective.* Int J Health Serv, 2014. **44**(3): p. 567-92.

3.   Rosenstein, A.H., *Strategies to Enhance Physician Engagement*. J Med Pract Manage, 2015. **31**(2): p. 113-6.

4.   Sally Hulks, N.W., Marcus Powell, Chris Ham and Hugh Alderwick, *Leading across the health and care system.* 2017.

5.   Senge, P.M., *The Fifth Discipline: The art and practice of the learning organization: Second edition*. Random House Business Books.

6.   Institute for Healthcare Improvement. *Quality Improvement Essentials Toolkit*. 2017; Available from: http://www.ihi.org/resources/Pages/Tools/Quality-Improvement-Essentials-Toolkit.aspx.

7.   Olson, K.D., *Physician Burnout—A Leading Indicator of Health System Performance? - Mayo Clinic Proceedings.* Mayo Clinic Proceedings, 2017. 92(11): p. 3.

8.   VIA_Institute. *Character Strengths, Character Building Experts: VIA Character*. 2018; Available from: http://www.viacharacter.org/www/.

9.   Plsek, P.E. and T. Wilson, *Complexity, leadership, and management in healthcare organisations.* 2001.

10. Plsek, P.E., *The challenge of complexity in health care*. 2001, BMJ.

11. Beyondblue *National Mental Health Survey of Doctors and Medical Students*. 2013.

12. Wible, P. *What I've learned from 687 doctor suicides*. DoctorPortal Blog, 2018.

13. Catalyst, N. *Physician Burnout: The Root of the Problem and the Path to Solutions*. 2017.

14. ACSQHC. *Healthcare Associated Infection*. 2017; Available from: https://www.safetyandquality.gov.au/our-work/healthcare-associated-infection/.

15. Committee on Quality of Health Care in America., *To Err Is Human/ Building a Safer Health System*, ed. I.o. Medicine. 2000.

16. ICHOM, *what matters most - Patient Outcomes and the Transformation of Health Care*. 2016. p. 73.

Chapter 9

1. Grube, M.E., *Making the Case for Virtual Healthcare*. Healthcare Executive, 2015(March/April 2015): p. 3.

2. Hood, L. *P4Medicine Institute*. 2012 JAN 2018]; Available from: http://www.p4mi.org/p4medicine.

3. Elbert, N.J., et al., *Effectiveness and cost-effectiveness of ehealth interventions in somatic diseases: a systematic review of systematic reviews and meta-analyses*. J Med Internet Res, 2014. 16(4): p. e110.

4. Prof. Branko Celler, D.M.V., Dr. Ross Sparks, Dr. Jane Li, Dr. Surya Nepal, Dr. Julian Jang-Jaccard, Mr. Simon McBride, and Dr. Rajiv Jayasena. *Home Monitoring Of Chronic Disease For Aged Care*. 2016 16/08/2017 7:03:00 AM; Available from: https://www.csiro.au/ en/Research/BF/Areas/Digital-health/Improving-access/Home-monitoring.

5. Minion, L., *Australian in-home care provider launches world-first holographic doctor*. Healthcare IT News, 2017. 03 OCT 17.

6. Gurman, M., *Alexa-enabled glasses set for debut*, in *Australian Financial Review*. 2018: Australia.

7. HealthTap. *HealthTap - Ask doctors now and get immediate help for free 24/7 - Advice, prescriptions, reminders, and more*. 2017.

8. HealthTap. *The world's first Health Operating System*. 2017.

9. Tero Koivisto, O.L., Tero Hurnanen, Mojtaba Jafari Tadi, Eero Lehtonen, Tuija Vasankari, Antti Saraste, Tuomas Kiviniemi, Juhani Airaksinen, Mikko Pänkäälä *Detecting indications of acute myocardial infarction using smartphone only solution*. European Congress on e-Cardiology & e-Health, 2016.

10. Langston, J. *New UW app can detect sleep apnea events via smartphone.* UW News, 2015.

11. Powick, A. *Opinion: Reflections of a health consumer with greater expectations.* Pulse+IT, 2018.

Chapter 10

1. Barry, M.J. and S. Edgman-Levitan, *Shared Decision Making — The Pinnacle of Patient-Centered Care.* N Engl J Med, 2012. **366**(March 1): p. 2.

2. Ayala, D.M.L. *The Root of All Satisfaction - Patients Want Caregivers Who Provide Information and Compassion.* PG Snapshot, 2017.

3. Smith, M., et al., *Engaging Patients, Families, and Communities,* in *Best Care at Lower Cost: The Path to Continuously Learning Health Care in America.,* Committee on the Learning Health Care System in America, Editor. 2013, National Academies Press (US).

4. Torpie, K., *Customer service vs. Patient care.* Patient Experience Journal, 2014. **1**(2): p. 3.

5. Garrett, J., *Effective Perioperative Communication to Enhance Patient Care- ClinicalKey.* AORN, 2016. 104(2): p. 111-120.

6. Haikerwal, M., Dobb, G., Ahmed, T. *Safe Handover: Safe Patients.* 2007.

7. ACSQHC. *Clinical Handover.* 2017; Available from: https://www. safetyandquality.gov.au/our-work/clinical-communications/clinical-handover/.

8. Collier, M. and L.M. Basham *Patient loyalty: It's up for grabs.* 2016.

9. Brian Kalis, J.F., Adam Burke, Marc Warren *Losing Patience: Why Healthcare Providers Need to Up Their Mobile Game.* 2015.

10. DiJulius, J., *The Customer Service Revolution: Overthrow Conventional Business, Inspire Employees, and Change the World.* 2015, Austin, Texas, USA: Greenleaf Book Group.

11. Bisognano, M., et al. *A Vision for "What Matters to You?".* [Text and

Video] 2018 [cited 2018; Available from: http://www.ihi.org/Topics/ WhatMatters/Pages/default.aspx.

12.   Bhattacharjee, A. and a. Dana, *People Think Companies Can't Do Good and Make Money. Can Companies Prove Them Wrong?* Harvard Business Review, 2017.

13.   RitzCarlton, L., *Patient Experience Impacts Safety* 2015, The Ritz-Carlton. p. When healthcare organizations become more patient-centric they empower employees and increase engagement, improve the patient experience and improve safety saving lives.

14.   PressGaneyAssociates *Total Patient Experience, Not Just Satisfaction Scores, Tied to Quality*. PG Snapshot, 2017. 16.

15.   AAPL/ BI. *Connected: Improving The Patient-Physician Relationship — And Health Care Itself — Through Communication*. A collaboration of the American Association for Physician Leadership® and The Beryl Institute. DEC 2017

16.   Gleeson, H., et al., *Systematic review of approaches to using patient experience data for quality improvement in healthcare settings*. BMJ Open, 2016. **6**(8).

Chapter 11

1.   Joseph Dwyer, S.J., and Sylvia Vriesendorp, *Occasional Paper: An Urgent Call to Professionalize Leadership and Management Health Care Worldwide*. Management Sciences for Health, 2006. 4: p. 31.

2.   Chase, D. *Healthcare: Unstoppable Force Meets Immovable Object*. HIT Consultant, 2016.

3.   Editorial, *The New Marketplace of Health Care - Impacts and Incentives of Payment Reform*. NEJM, 2017.

4.   Taylor, M. and S. Hill *Consumer expectations and healthcare in Australia*. 2015.

5.   Victoria, D. *Better Quality, Better Health Care: A Safety and Quality Improvement Framework for Victorian Health Services*. 2018.

6.   Berwick, D.M., *Developing and testing changes in delivery of care.* Ann Intern Med, 1998. 128(8): p. 651-6.

7.   McCormack, B., et al., *Getting evidence into practice: the meaning of 'context'.* J Adv Nurs, 2002. 38(1): p. 94-104.

8.   Kaplan, H.C., et al., *The influence of context on quality improvement success in health care: a systematic review of the literature.* Milbank Q, 2010. **88**(4): p. 500-59.

9.   Jorm, C., *Clinician engagement: Scoping paper.* 2016.

10.   Gawande, A., *The Checklist Manifesto.* 2009.

11.   Marshall, M., *Applying quality improvement approaches to health care.* BMJ, 2009. 339(b3411).

12.   Oxman, A.D., et al., *No magic bullets: a systematic review of 102 trials of interventions to improve professional practice.* Cmaj, 1995. 153(10): p. 1423-31.

13.   Donaldson, L.S. *Report of the High Level Group on Clinical Effectiveness.* 2007.

14.   Greenhalgh, T., et al., *Diffusion of innovations in service organizations: systematic review and recommendations.* Milbank Q, 2004. 82(4): p. 581-629.

15.   Plsek, P.E. and T. Wilson, *Complexity, leadership, and management in healthcare organisations.* 2001.

16.   Damschroder, L.J., et al., *Fostering implementation of health services research findings into practice: a consolidated framework for advancing implementation science.* Implement Sci, 2009. 4: p. 50.

Chapter 12

1.   Nikhil R. SahniAnuraag ChigurupatiBob Kocher, M.M.C., *How the U.S. Can Reduce Waste in Health Care Spending by $1 Trillion.* HBR, 2015.

2.   CommonwealthFund. *International Health Care System Profiles.* 2016; Available from: http://international.commonwealthfund.org/.

3.   Britnell, M., *In Search of the Perfect Health System.* 2015: Palgrave Macmillan. Kindle Edition.

4. Booske, B., *Different Perspectives For Assigning Weights To Determinants Of Health*. 2010, University of Wisconsin.

5. Resar RK, G.F., Kabcenell A, Bones C *Hospital Inpatient Waste Identification Tool*. Institute for Healthcare Improvement, 2017.

6. International Consortium for Health Oucomes Measurement. *What matters most - Patient Outcomes and the Transformation of Health Care*. 2016. p. 73.

7. Haughom, J., *Quality Improvement in Healthcare: 5 Deming Principles*. 2016.

8. ACSQHC. *Second Australian Atlas of Healthcare Variation 2017*. 2017 [cited 2017 17 Dec 17]; Available from: https://www.safetyandquality. gov.au/national-priorities/.

9. Institute for Healthcare Improvement. *Quality Improvement Essentials Toolkit*. 2017; Available from: http://www.ihi.org/resources/Pages/ Tools/Quality-Improvement-Essentials-Toolkit.aspx.

10. Kennedy, L., *Hidden Hospital Hazards: Saving Lives and Improving Margins*. Busybird Publishing, Melbourne, Australia.

Chapter 13

1. WHO *Systems Thinking for Health Systems Strengthening*. 2009.

2. Scrivens, J. *Is collaboration the new innovation?* HRM, 2016.

3. Burrell, L., *Co-Creating the Employee Experience*. Harvard Business Review, 2018. 96(2): p. 5.

4. Adam, T. and D.d. Savigny, *Systems thinking for health systems strengthening in LMICs: Seizing the opportunity*. Health Policy and Planning, 2012.

5. Craig Wright, K.P., *Discussion: New Thinking Leads to Better Transitions*. Physician Leadership Journal, 2018. 5(1): p. 3.

6. Bennett, N. and G.J. Lemoine, *What VUCA Really Means for You*. Harvard Business Review, 2014.

Chapter 14

1. ICHOM, *What matters most - Patient Outcomes and the Transformation of Health Care.* 2016. p. 73.

2. Ayala, D.M.L. *The Root of All Satisfaction - Patients Want Caregivers Who Provide Information and Compassion.* PG Snapshot, 2017.

3. WHO *Systems Thinking for Health Systems Strengthening.* 2009.

4. Burrell, L., *Co-Creating the Employee Experience.* Harvard Business Review, 2018. 96(2): p. 5.

5. Gregersen, H., *Better Brainstorming.* Harvard Business Review, 2018. 96(2): p. 8.

6. Snyder, B., *The Best Patient Experience: Helping Physicians Improve Care, Satisfaction, and Scores.* 2016, Chicago: Health Administration Press.

Chapter 15

1. Flanigan, B. and S. Thomas. *Six physician alignment strategies for health systems.* 2018; Available from: https://www2.deloitte.com/us/en/pages/life-sciences-and-health-care/articles/physician-alignment-strategy-health-system-executive-survey-findings.html.

2. Dyke, M.V. *Elevating Leadership: Insights and Strategies for Healthcare Leaders.* 2016.

3. Brown, B., *3 Steps to Prioritize Clinical Quality Improvement in Healthcare.* HealthCatalyst, 2014.

4. Cummings, E., et al. *An Evidence-Based Review and Training Resource on Smooth Patient Flow.* 2012 [cited 2018 Feb]; Available from: http://www.health.nsw.gov.au/wohp/Documents/UTAS-patient-flow-evidence.pdf.

5. Haughom, J., *Quality Improvement in Healthcare: 5 Deming Principles.* 2016.

6. Wolfe, A., *Institute of Medicine Report: Crossing the Quality Chasm: A New Health Care System for the 21st Century.* http://dx.doi.org/10.1177/152715440100200312, 2016.

7. Swensen, S., A. Kabcenell, and T. Shanafelt, *Physician-Organization*

Collaboration Reduces Physician Burnout and Promotes Engagement: The Mayo Clinic Experience. J Healthc Manag, 2016. 61(2): p. 105-27.

8.   Catalyst, N. *Physician Burnout: The Root of the Problem and the Path to Solutions.* 2017.

9.   Brach, K., *Erika Hall*, in *Offscreen*. 2018, Kai Brach: Melbourne. p. 18.

Chapter 16

1.   Tucker, R. *5G vs NBN: Next-gen mobile network will be a convenient but expensive alternative.* The Conversation, 2017. DOI: http://www.abc.net.au/news/2017-10-25/5g-vs-nbn-mobile-network-convenient-but-expensive-alternative/9083746.

2.   IMT. *Digital Health Trends.* 2017 2017-12-29; Available from: https://imtinnovation.com/digital-health/.

3.   McCauley, R., *Digital Biology: Reading, Writing and Hacking DNA*, in *SingularityU Summit*, SingularityU, Editor. 2018: Sydney, Australia.

4.   Kraft, D. *Future of Health & Medicine.* 2018; Available from: http://singularityuaustraliasummit.com/schedule.

5.   Yiersly, L. *AI for Humans.* 2018; Available from: http://singularityu-australiasummit.com/schedule.

6.   Rizzo, A.S. and L.-P. Morency. *SimSensei.* 2011; Available from: http://ict.usc.edu/prototypes/simsensei/.

7.   Urban, T., *The Artificial Intelligence Revolution: Part 1 - Wait But Why.* 2015, @waitbutwhy.

8.   UniversityMelbourne. *SocialNUI: Microsoft Centre for Social Natural User Interfaces at The University of Melbourne.* 2018; Available from: http://www.socialnui.unimelb.edu.au/#research.

9.   Multiple, *The biggest healthcare breaches of 2017.* Healthcare IT News, 2017 from http://www.healthcareitnews.com/slideshow/biggest-healthcare-breaches-2017-so-far.

Conclusion

1.   http://www.drucker.institute/rankings-background/

INDEX

www.ingramcontent.com/pod-product-compliance
Lightning Source LLC
Chambersburg PA
CBHW060540210326
41519CB00014B/3289